Rebecoming

Become Free from What Holds You Back in Life and Return to Who You Truly Are

Steve Roche & Cilla Hall

REBECOMING

First published in 2025 by Dragonwood

ISBN: 978-1-9162493-8-7

A CIP catalogue record for this book is available from the British Library.

Dragonwood www.dragonwood.co.uk

Printed and bound in the UK.

DEDICATION

To everyone who has shown unconditional love.

CONTENTS

FOREWORD

This foreword is different. It wasn't written by a single expert or authority. Instead, it carries the voices of people just like you, whom we have personally worked with—individuals who felt stuck, lost, or disconnected from themselves and chose to embark on the journey of rebecoming. Their collective wisdom speaks to what is possible when you decide to come home to yourself.

We each had that moment when we realised we were living someone else's story. For some of us, it was pursuing achievements to prove a point to the doubters. For others, it was getting into unloving relationships at a young age to escape life at home, or putting on a mask of success to hide our fears and insecurities. And beneath it all, many of us were carrying the weight of old wounds—years of abuse, neglect, or pain that shaped who we thought we had to be. We looked in the mirror and wondered: 'Is this really me? Is this what my life is meant to be like?'

What we discovered is that this feeling of disconnection wasn't a flaw—it was an awakening. It was our souls calling us back home to ourselves.

When you pick up this book, you are joining us on this pivotal journey. Like us, you are ready to question everything: the stories you have been told about who you should be, the emotional baggage weighing down your spirit, the limiting beliefs that keep you small, and the external voices that drown out your inner wisdom.

We learned that rebecoming isn't about becoming someone new. It is about peeling away the layers of conditioning, healing the wounds that made us hide our true selves, and rediscovering the authentic person who has been there all along. Every challenge we faced, every pattern we repeated, and every moment we felt lost was actually preparing us for this transformation.

This journey asked us to be brave. We examined beliefs we had never questioned, felt emotions we had long suppressed, and released identities that once felt essential to our survival. But with each layer we shed, we felt lighter. With each story we rewrote, we felt more powerful. With each step toward authenticity, we felt more alive.

We discovered that the world needs who we really are—not who we have been pretending to be.

From all of us who have walked this path using the teachings of this book, we say welcome to your journey back to yourself. Welcome to your rebecoming.

BEFORE YOU BEGIN

This book you are holding, and the Head, Heart & Soul business we have created—they were born from what we went through. We went through the mess, the pain, the confusion of letting our real selves emerge, and from that experience came a desire to help others do the same. Every word, every tool, every piece of wisdom we share comes from walking this path ourselves.

The journey we are inviting you on is not about self-improvement or transformation in the way you might think. It is about awakening to who you have always been. All those years of trying to be what others expected, of carrying emotional baggage that was never yours to hold - that is what falls away.

We promise you this: the real you, waiting to emerge, is worth every difficult step it takes to find. And when you do, you will understand why everything had to happen precisely as it did. You are not broken. You are not too much or not enough. You are simply ready to become who you have always been underneath it all.

This is for the real you—the one who has been waiting all along. You can do this.

This book is just the beginning. For more tools, guidance, and support as you continue your journey of letting go and rebecoming, visit us at www.headheartandsoul.co.uk.

Steve Roche & Cilla Hall

OUR STORIES OF REBECOMING

Cilla's Story

I am a '70s child, a twin and a younger sister. My mum was one of the strongest people I knew, bringing us all up alone, but she carried a lot of wounds, so she wasn't the most emotionally available person to be around. This, I now realise, was the very basis of my own emotional baggage—those early unmet needs for emotional safety and connection that would shape my protective system for decades to come.

Growing up, I was quiet and happy in my own company. At some point, I realised I felt different from many people in my life—siblings, school friends, and work colleagues (I started working at 13 years old)—but I had no idea why, so I kept trying to be like everyone else to fit in. I was already living from limiting beliefs about who I was supposed to be, rather than honouring the real me.

In secondary school, I got bullied, which really knocked my confidence. I had no self-worth and no one at home to talk to. I became closed off to myself, constantly criticising myself and putting myself last, while making sure that I would look after everyone else, putting them first, always being nice and protecting them whenever I could, hoping that behaviour would mean that people would like me. My protection system had kicked into full gear—if I could just be perfect enough, helpful enough, maybe I would finally feel loved and safe.

Deep down, I knew I craved love. I wanted to feel special. I thought I could get it externally, so I dated and married, but I failed to work on myself. The broken girl was all I could offer, and it was never enough. I was seeking external validation instead of building the relationship with myself that I truly needed.

I started my rebecoming journey back in 2012. At first, I was scared and kept running away. I would try something, a session where someone did some healing work with me, and I would feel good, but then my self-sabotage would kick in, and I would run again. It was like one step forward, two steps back. I kept making excuses for why I couldn't get somewhere or meet someone. Then blocks would appear, like when one of my children wasn't feeling well, so I had to stay home. This went on for a few years, but each time I allowed myself to go somewhere, meet someone, take part in a session, I began to see changes in myself. I started thinking differently about my life. I began to see there was another way. Eventually, I realised that I couldn't step back anymore. It was like I had crossed an invisible line, and I didn't want to be the person I was. I was beginning to like the person I was becoming. My inner knowing was finally becoming stronger than my fear.

The road ahead was long. It was exhausting and frustrating. I would be pushed by the person who was guiding me, and I wanted to scream at them and ask them how the hell did they know how I was feeling—but of course, they did because they had done this work on themselves too. The work was very demanding, leaving me feeling down and with low energy, but I began to realise that I didn't have to stay there. I understood that it was OK to have a day or two or three where I allowed the release, then I would give myself permission to pick myself up again, enjoy my higher energy and the levelling up that had occurred. I was learning the messy, non-linear nature of healing and how to be gentle with myself through the process.

I think the most important thing I have learned is that growth does not happen when things are going well. Growth happens when you are being triggered, in pain, or dealing with loss. When things are what you would call bad, that is when you learn the lessons that are being shown to you. When you come through that period, you can look back and see how far you have come, and celebrate. I learned to see my triggers and challenges not as evidence that I was broken, but as opportunities for deeper healing and expansion.

This is not a journey for the faint of heart, but it is a journey worth taking if you feel stuck, unhappy, and yearn for more than life is currently offering. Be brave and do what most of us don't—put yourself first, because when you work on yourself, it will have a ripple effect on everyone in your life, and that I can confirm as a fact. Your healing contributes to the healing of everyone around you.

All my love, Cilla x

Steve's Story

I was a quiet child. Speaking up was hard. I thought I was boring, and who would want to hear what I had to say? I felt that I wasn't like everyone else and didn't matter, that somehow, I was worth less than everyone else around me.

As a child, I had very few friends and felt like an outsider, so I kept myself to myself. I spent most of my time in my room listening to the radio and reading books. When I looked in the mirror, I thought I was ugly too—just another reason to hide away.

But deep down, I wanted to belong. I remember taking my football to the park, hoping to join in when I saw boys playing a match. But I was always too shy to ask, so I would just stand on the sidelines watching, sometimes for ages. Plus, I never felt I was good enough to play with them anyway. Generally, in life, I didn't have much confidence.

I was really sensitive. I could feel what everyone around me was feeling - their worries, their anger, their sadness. It all hit me at once and felt like too much. I couldn't tell where their feelings ended and mine began. So, I escaped into my own world - anywhere but the real world that felt too intense. When emotions got too much, I would go into my head and try to think my way through feelings or numb them out instead of actually feeling them.

As an adult, I became better at dealing with my shyness. I made some friends, got a job, and eventually did all the usual stuff. But I always felt something was off. Somehow, I knew a different person was living deep inside me, waiting to emerge. I could sense it, like a constant whisper beneath the surface of my everyday life.

Then, on an ordinary day a few years ago, everything changed. Out of nowhere, I felt this warm, glowing sensation centred around my heart. I had never experienced anything like it and had no idea what was happening. It was as if a door that had been locked tight for decades suddenly swung open. Something fundamental had shifted, though I didn't understand what.

It became clear a few weeks later. Something unexpected began and continued over the next several years - all the emotional pain I had buried and numbed out started rising to the surface. It wasn't all at once - it came in waves. Every old hurt, every time I had felt worthless, every moment of being left out - you name it, it all came back demanding to be felt. It was messy, painful, and confusing.

But I had always been curious, always eager to learn. Through my searching, I discovered an ancient writing practice that helped me pour out all the words I had never been able to speak aloud. I researched other wisdom traditions as well, finding tools to face and process my emotional wounds rather than run from them. Some days, I wanted to make it all stop, but the boy who used to hide in his room had nowhere left to escape to.

Slowly, things started to shift. That sensitivity I had always struggled with? It turned out to be useful. As I improved at managing my own feelings, I discovered that I could also help others with theirs. My voice - the one I thought was worthless - started to resonate with people who felt as lost as I once did. I am still learning, but I now see that those things I thought were my biggest challenges turned out to be great gifts.

I have learned through all of this that there is a real you underneath everything—underneath the pain, the protection, the masks we wear to fit in. That whisper I felt beneath the surface of my everyday life? It was my real self, patiently waiting all those years to emerge. And when it finally did, everything began to make sense.

Steve

INTRODUCTION

'Maybe the journey isn't so much about becoming anything. Maybe it's about unbecoming everything that isn't really you, so you can be who you were meant to be in the first place.' - Paulo Coelho

Have you ever felt like you have lost touch with your true self? Do you find yourself weighed down by emotional baggage, confined by societal expectations, or simply going through the motions without deep purpose or fulfilment? If so, you are not alone. Many of us, especially in midlife, yearn to break free from the masks we wear and rediscover who we truly are.

This book is your invitation to embark on a profound journey of Rebecoming. 'Re' means to return, and 'becoming' speaks to transformation. But this is not about becoming someone different. It is about returning to who you truly are—peeling away the layers of who you thought you needed to be, so you can rediscover the authentic self that has been there all along.

Throughout this book, we will explore a powerful truth that might just change everything: ***Your inner world is the only thing that truly affects your outer reality.***

It is not your job, relationships, or circumstances that ultimately determine your life experience. It is what's going on inside you—your thoughts, beliefs, and emotions. We all have a self-concept that acts as a filter, colouring everything we see and do. However, the key is that this self-concept is not always based on truth. It is often shaped by past experiences, especially painful ones, creating what we call emotional baggage.

Think of this baggage as a heavy cloud hanging over you, filled with old hurts, fears, and limiting beliefs. It weighs you down, keeps you playing small, and prevents you from reaching your full potential. But—and this is crucial—this cloud is not actually part of who you are. Every time you find the courage to face your fears or work through pain, pieces of that cloud break away. As it clears, the real you begins to shine through.

What makes this book different

Unlike many modern self-help books that rely on the latest trends, this book draws from ancient wisdom traditions that have stood the test of time. Buddhism, Taoism, Stoicism, and other traditions offer profound insights into the human experience and powerful tools for transformation. We have become disconnected from these timeless truths, often searching for quick fixes instead. But the journey of Rebecoming is not about adopting new beliefs—it is about rediscovering the ancient wisdom that already lies within you.

This is not about positive thinking or ignoring reality. It is about seeing reality clearly, without the distortions of past pain. It is about reclaiming your power to shape your life from the inside out.

Your journey ahead

In this book, you will discover:

- Where your self-concept comes from and how to transform it.
- Practical techniques for recognising and releasing emotional baggage.
- Ancient wisdom practices adapted for modern life.
- How to rewrite limiting stories and create an empowering self-concept.
- Ways to reconnect with the real you

As you become more 'you,' some people might resist the changes. However, remember that the most genuine connections come from being your authentic self. By letting go of what is not truly you, you open the door to deeper, more meaningful relationships.

An invitation to transform

Real learning—the kind that changes you—requires engagement. Don't just read these pages; wrestle with them. Question them. See how they fit with what you know and believe. This journey requires you to be open, ready to learn, and willing to adapt and change.

Throughout this book, you will discover practical tools and exercises to support your transformation. We have created 'Your Rebecoming Toolkit'—a reference guide at the back of this book containing quick-access versions of every practice. This makes it easy to return to any technique without having to search through chapters.

Are you ready to lighten your load and step into a more vibrant, fulfilling version of yourself? If you are nodding your head right now, then turn the page. Your journey of Rebecoming starts now.

Welcome to this transformative path. May this book be your trusted companion as you navigate the ups and downs of returning to who you truly are. The truth is simple: the real you is not your busy, fearful, pleasure-seeking mind. It is your calm, loving, and joyous soul.

How to Use This Book

This book is designed as a transformative journey, and we have structured it to guide you step by step. In Part One, we will help you recognise what has been holding you back. Part Two takes you deeper into timeless wisdom traditions, showing how ancient teachings can illuminate your path forward. Part Three is where everything comes together, offering practical ways to integrate these insights into your daily life and step fully into who you are meant to be.

If you want all the exercises from the various chapters in Part 3 gathered together in one place, you can download The Rebecoming Toolkit from our website as a PDF at:

- **www.headheartandsoul.co.uk/rebecoming-toolkit**

There is no right or wrong way to use this book - some people read it straight through first, while others pause to practice as they go. Trust yourself to know what works best for you. This is not a book to rush through; it is designed to be a resource you can return to again and again as you continue your journey of rebecoming.

PART 1: WHAT HOLDS YOU BACK IN LIFE

You might think that what is keeping you stuck is something you lack - maybe more money, a better job, or the perfect relationship. However, the truth is that what is really holding you back is already within you or around you. It is not about what you don't have, but about what you are carrying and how you are showing up in life.

Throughout this journey, we will explore nine core issues that block most people from living their fullest lives:

- *Avoiding Responsibility* - This is when you let life happen to you instead of taking charge of your choices; you give away your power to create change.
- *Being Conditioned* - Understanding that various systems and influences shape your choices without you noticing, from family expectations to cultural norms that tell you who to be.
- *Emotional Baggage* - All those past hurts and unresolved traumas weigh you down like rocks in a backpack, making it nearly impossible to move forward freely.
- *Misunderstanding Love* - Learning that society's distorted messages about love and relationships often lead you to chase connections that do not fulfil you or reflect what love truly means.
- *Lack of Self-Care* - How neglecting your own needs leaves you empty, resentful, and disconnected from your true self.
- *Money Blocks* - How your relationship with finances might be tangled in fear, shame, or limiting beliefs that prevent you from experiencing financial peace of mind.
- *Negative Energy* - Realising that the energy you carry and surround yourself with affects everything - when it is low, creating positive change feels nearly impossible.
- *An Inner Divide* - This is when your masculine and feminine aspects are out of balance, it creates internal conflict that keeps you from feeling whole.
- *A Feeling of Emptiness* - When living without meaning and a sense of purpose leaves you adrift, going through motions rather than creating a life that genuinely lights you up.

The good news is that transforming your life is not about acquiring something new. It is about becoming aware of these hidden factors and consciously choosing to change them. In the following chapters, we will explore each of these issues in depth, uncover how they operate in your life, and provide practical tools to break free.

Your journey of rebecoming is about reclaiming your power and using it to create the life you truly desire, not the one other people have prescribed for you. Fear-driven patterns will hold you back, but connecting with your soul will elevate you beyond what you thought possible.

THE HIDDEN COST OF NOT TAKING RESPONSIBILITY

How often do you catch yourself saying things like 'It's not my fault' or 'I had no choice' or 'There's nothing I can do about it'? Most of us have. It is natural to want to distance ourselves from things that are not going well in our lives. But every time you do this, you are giving away your power to change things. When you do not take responsibility for your life, you are essentially handing over the keys to your happiness to others and circumstances. You become a passenger in your own life, watching it unfold from the backseat instead of taking the wheel.

When you do not take responsibility, several things happen. First, you stay stuck. If nothing is your fault or responsibility, then nothing is in your power to change. It is like being in a room with all the doors locked, complaining about being trapped, while holding the key in your pocket the whole time.

Second, you give your power away to others. When you blame your boss for your career frustrations, your partner for your relationship problems, or your parents for your emotional issues, you are essentially saying, 'These people have more control over my life than I do.' Is that really true? Is that how you want to live?

Third, you miss out on growth opportunities. Every challenge in your life is an opportunity to learn, adapt, and become stronger. But when you are busy pointing fingers at others or making excuses, you cannot see these opportunities. It is like having a box full of seeds in your garden but never planting them because you are too busy complaining about the weather.

Fourth, your relationships suffer. Nobody likes being around someone who constantly makes excuses or blames others. It is exhausting. Additionally, when you fail to take responsibility, you cannot build genuine intimacy or trust with others, as you are not being honest with them or yourself.

If we are being honest, not taking responsibility can feel comfortable in the short term. It is easier to blame others or circumstances than to face our own role in creating our current situation. It is more comfortable to make excuses than to make changes.

But this comfort is an illusion. It is like taking painkillers for a broken leg without getting it set - you might feel better temporarily, but you are not addressing the real problem. And the longer you avoid taking responsibility, the more painful and difficult it becomes to finally face reality.

One of the biggest traps we fall into is the 'victim story.' This is the narrative we tell ourselves about why things are the way they are and why we can't change them. Maybe your victim story is about how life is unfair, or how you never got the opportunities others did, or how circumstances are stacked against you.

The problem with these stories is not that they are not true; it is that they keep you stuck. They become self-fulfilling prophecies. When you believe you are powerless to change your life, you stop trying. And when you stop trying, nothing changes, which reinforces your belief that you are powerless.

We then need to examine the excuses we make. Excuses might seem harmless at first glance, but they come with a steep price tag that affects every area of your life. Each time you make an excuse, you rob yourself of your personal power and keep yourself playing small instead of stepping into your full potential. These excuses become barriers that prevent you from learning and growing from your experiences. Over time, they chip away at your self-respect, as you know, deep down, that you are not being honest with yourself. Others notice too, and every excuse erodes their trust in you bit by bit.

Perhaps most costly of all, excuses become invisible walls that block you from achieving your dreams. Every excuse you make is like putting another brick in the wall between you and the life you want to live.

If any of this is resonating with you, consider this your wake-up call. The life you are living right now is the result of countless choices - some conscious, some unconscious. Some of these choices may have been made for you when you were younger, but now that you are an adult, you can make them yourself. Now you get to choose. You get to choose whether to stay stuck in old patterns or create new ones that serve your growth. You get to choose whether to keep making excuses that keep you comfortable or start making the changes that will transform your life. You get to choose whether to blame others for your circumstances or take full responsibility for your life and reclaim your power. The choice is yours - and it is a choice you make every single day, with every thought, word, and action.

Later in this book, we will dive deep into how to take full ownership of every aspect of your life. But for now, just notice where you might be giving away your power. Notice where you are making excuses or playing the victim. Notice where you are blaming others instead of taking responsibility. Because the truth is that your life is your responsibility. No one is coming to save you. No one can make it all better. And that is actually good news because it means you have the power to change things.

The choice is yours. Will you continue to give your power away? Or are you ready to take responsibility for your life? Remember - taking responsibility is not about blame. It is about power. When you truly understand this, everything can change.

YOU ARE BEING CONDITIONED

Have you ever felt like you are not fully in charge of your own life? Like invisible forces are guiding your decisions, shaping your beliefs, and influencing your behaviour? If so, you are not alone. We are all subject to conditioning in ways we might not even realise. At the heart of it all is a simple truth: people, businesses, and institutions want something from you. They want your energy, your attention, your time, and often, your money. In today's world, these resources are incredibly valuable, and there is fierce competition to capture them.

The conditioned self is the version of you that has been shaped and programmed by external influences throughout your life. It is a collection of beliefs, behaviours, and responses that you have absorbed and internalised from your family, education, culture, media, and society—often without conscious awareness or choice.

This conditioning begins in childhood when you are like a sponge, absorbing messages about:

- who you should be
- what success looks like
- how you should behave
- what to value and believe
- what is possible or impossible for you

Over time, these external messages become your internal voice. You might think these perspectives are your own, but many are actually programming you have received from others. The conditioned self then operates on autopilot, making choices based on this programming rather than your authentic desires.

Society's Invisible Rulebook

Society has many unwritten rules about how you should live your life. These expectations can subtly control you.

Think about how society tells men and women to behave differently. Maybe you have felt pressure to act a certain way just because of your gender. You might have caught yourself holding back tears as a man because 'real men don't cry,' or felt guilty as a woman for prioritising your career over starting a family.

Then there is how your culture defines success. Does it paint a picture of the good life as having a big house, a fancy car, or a high-powered job? These expectations might be pushing you towards goals that are not really yours. You may find yourself climbing the corporate ladder, chasing a bigger salary, when deep down, you would be happier pursuing a creative passion or working for a nonprofit.

Societal expectations also create unspoken timelines for our lives. Have you ever felt behind because you are not married or don't own a home by a certain age? You might feel a gnawing anxiety as you approach 30 without a long-term partner, or feel embarrassed to admit you are still renting at 40, even if you are perfectly happy with your life choices.

These societal norms become part of your conditioned self, creating automatic responses and judgments that may not align with your true values.

The Subtle Art of Marketing Manipulation

Companies spend billions trying to influence your choices, and they have perfected the art of it. Their goal? To control your behaviour as a consumer, often in ways you might not even notice, by programming your conditioned self. Ads often create false needs, making you feel like you are missing out if you don't have their product. That latest smartphone? Suddenly, your current one seems outdated. That new fashion trend? Now your wardrobe feels boring. It is a constant cycle of creating discontent and then offering a solution for a price.

Commercials employ clever emotional manipulation through catchy music, compelling imagery, and heartwarming stories to connect their products with positive emotions. They are not just selling a product. They are selling a lifestyle, an identity, and a solution to your problems. And in the digital age, targeted ads use your browsing history to show you products you are more likely to buy, creating an echo chamber of consumerism. Your social media feed becomes a personalised shopping catalogue, reinforcing the conditioned responses that marketers want to instil in you.

Family and Peer Pressure

The people closest to you can have a considerable influence on your conditioned self, often more than you realise. This is another form of external control, one that can be particularly hard to recognise and resist because it comes from people you care about. Your parents might have strong ideas about your career path or who you should marry, and their expectations become part of your conditioning. Maybe you chose your college course to please them, or you are hesitant to introduce them to a partner who does not fit their idea of who you should be with.

Your friends' opinions on fashion, music, or lifestyle can shape your own choices, sometimes without you even noticing. You might find yourself adopting their tastes or habits, not because you genuinely prefer them, but because your conditioned self has learned that fitting in is safe and comfortable.

And underlying it all might be a fear of disappointment—you find yourself making choices just to avoid letting others down, even if those choices don't match with your true desires. This fear becomes a powerful conditioned response, keeping you on a path that others have chosen for you.

Technology Hijacking Your Brain

While the forms of conditioning we have discussed so far have been around for generations, modern technology has introduced new, highly sophisticated methods of programming the conditioned self. The digital world is designed to keep you hooked on your devices, often at the expense of your time, attention, and even your mental health.

Have you ever wondered why it is so hard to put down your phone, or why you keep scrolling through social media even when you meant to go to bed an hour ago? At the heart of this conditioning is dopamine—your brain's 'feel good' chemical that is released when you experience something pleasurable.

Technology companies have become experts at exploiting this system. They use techniques like infinite scrolling, push notifications, autoplay features, and like buttons to trigger dopamine releases, conditioning your brain to crave these digital interactions.

The result? Your conditioned self develops automatic habits of reaching for your phone, checking notifications, and seeking digital validation. These behaviours become so ingrained that they feel like part of who you are, even though they are actually programmed responses.

Living on Autopilot

When you are unaware of this conditioning, you may find

yourself simply going through the motions of life. This is what living on autopilot looks like—letting your conditioned self guide your life instead of making conscious choices from your authentic self.

Think about how each form of conditioning we have discussed can contribute to this state:

- Society's expectations might have your conditioned self pursuing a career you don't really want because it is what is 'respectable' or 'secure.'
- Marketing manipulation could have your conditioned self spending money on things you don't need, trying to keep up with others or fill an emotional void.
- Family and peer pressure might keep your conditioned self in unfulfilling relationships because you are afraid of disappointing others or being alone.
- And technology might have conditioned you to check your phone hundreds of times a day, disconnecting you from real-world experiences and relationships.

It is like you are in a car, but your conditioned self is steering. The danger is that you could wake up one day and realise you have travelled far down a road you never intended to take.

Understanding these forms of conditioning is the first step towards breaking free from them. By recognising the difference between your real self and your conditioned responses, you can begin to make choices that truly align with who you are beneath the programming. It is OK if these external controls have influenced you. We all develop a conditioned self to some extent. The important thing is that you are now becoming aware of it. This awareness is your first step toward true freedom and authenticity.

Now that you see how conditioning shapes your thoughts, beliefs, and behaviours - from family patterns to social media algorithms - you might wonder, 'How do I break free and think for myself?' That is what we will explore in the corresponding chapter in Part 3. There, you will learn practical tools for recognising conditioning as it happens and choosing your own authentic responses instead of automatic reactions. For now, appreciate this new awareness. Seeing the invisible forces that influence you is the first step to reclaiming your power to choose.

THE BURDEN OF YOUR EMOTIONAL BAGGAGE

Think of emotional baggage as all the unhealed emotional wounds you have collected throughout your life that you haven't fully processed or let go of yet. It is like carrying around an invisible backpack that impacts how you think, feel, and act - often without you even realising it is there.

Your emotional baggage can manifest in various ways in your life, often revealing itself through your thoughts, emotions, and behaviours. You may find yourself becoming emotionally triggered by certain situations that remind you of past hurts, or struggle to trust others and open up in relationships. Perhaps you hold yourself back from opportunities because you are afraid of getting hurt, or you stay stuck in patterns of negative thinking and self-criticism. You may notice that you have trouble setting boundaries, carry around unexplained anxiety or sadness, or make decisions based on fear rather than what you really want. The weight of this baggage might even show up as a persistent feeling that you are not good enough or worthy of good things. While these patterns might seem disconnected on the surface, they are often different expressions of the same underlying emotional wounds that have not fully healed.

The thing about emotional baggage is that it often operates beneath the surface of your everyday awareness. You might not connect your current struggles or reactions to past experiences, but just like a heavy backpack weighs you down physically, emotional baggage can drain your energy, limit your choices, and prevent you from living life to the fullest.

The good news is that once you recognise your emotional baggage for what it is, you can start taking steps to heal those old wounds and lighten your load. You don't have to carry the weight of your past experiences forever.

What Emotional Wounds Are and How They Form

Think about the last time someone's words or actions really hurt you - the kind of hurt that stayed with you long after the moment passed. That lingering pain is what we call an emotional wound. You might be carrying several of these wounds without even realising it, each one shaping how you see yourself and the world around you.

But how exactly do these wounds form? Most of them actually

originate in childhood, when your brain and sense of self are still developing and you are most vulnerable to emotional injury. During these formative years, even seemingly small experiences can leave a lasting impact because you haven't yet developed the tools to process difficult emotional situations. Understanding this process is like turning on a light in a dark room - suddenly, you can see what has been there all along.

When an emotional wound forms, it starts with something that feels like too much to handle - what we can call a traumatic event. Sometimes these events are major and obvious, like being bullied throughout school or watching your parents go through a bitter divorce. At other times, they are more subtle, such as a teacher repeatedly ignoring your raised hand or a friend failing to show up when you really needed them. What makes something traumatic is not its size, but rather how overwhelming it feels to you in that moment.

If you have support and can process what happened in a healthy way, you may be able to move through these experiences without developing lasting wounds. However, if those feelings become stuck inside you, if you lack support, or if you are already feeling vulnerable, a wound can form. These wounds hit us hard, not so much because of what happened, but because of the meaning we give to what happened. When something painful occurs, our minds immediately try to make sense of it by connecting it to our deepest human needs - our need to feel safe, loved, valued, and to have a sense of belonging. The meaning we create often comes in the form of painful conclusions, such as 'This means I'm not safe,' 'I don't matter,' 'I'm not loved,' or 'I don't belong.'

These are not just fleeting thoughts in the moment; they become deep-seated beliefs that create lasting patterns in your life. You might find yourself believing certain things about yourself ('I'm not good enough'), creating protective behaviours ('I'll never let anyone see the real me'), repeating relationship patterns ('I always end up with people who let me down'), or even experiencing physical symptoms like anxiety, tension, and exhaustion.

The way you interpret new events is not random - it is shaped by everything you have experienced before, especially those early childhood wounds. It is like wearing invisible glasses that colour how you see every new situation. For instance, if you grew up feeling invisible in your family, someone not acknowledging you at a party might feel like massive rejection, reinforcing that old belief that you don't matter. But if you didn't form this emotional wound, you might just assume they were distracted and think nothing more of it.

The Meaning Behind Our Pain

At the heart of understanding emotional baggage are four basic needs we all share as humans: the need to feel safe, loved, accepted, and that we belong. These are not just nice-to-haves - they are essential for your emotional wellbeing. Particularly, the need to feel safe.

When you feel safe, it goes beyond just physical security. It means feeling emotionally secure enough to be yourself and trust the world around you. Love is not just about romantic relationships - it is about feeling worthy of affection from family, friends, and most importantly, yourself. Acceptance means feeling like you can be your true self without hiding parts of who you are. And belonging feeds our deep need to feel connected to something bigger than ourselves, whether that is family, community, or a cause we believe in.

When these fundamental needs are not met, it creates deep emotional pain. Imagine feeling like you are constantly walking on eggshells, or carrying around a belief that you are unlovable. Perhaps you think you have to wear a mask to be accepted, or that you are somehow different from everyone else and don't fit in anywhere. These feelings are not just uncomfortable - they can be overwhelming.

As Dr Gabor Maté explains, 'Trauma is not what happens to you, but what happens inside you.' This means that when something painful happens, it is not the event itself that creates the lasting wound - it is the meaning you give to it and how it connects to these core needs. For instance, a parent's criticism might be interpreted as 'I'm not good enough' (touching your need to feel that you matter), or being left out of a group might feel like 'I don't belong anywhere' (affecting your need for belonging).

These meanings often become deeply rooted in childhood, when you are most vulnerable and still developing your understanding of yourself and the world. During these formative years, even seemingly small experiences can leave lasting impressions because you haven't yet developed the emotional tools to process difficult situations. A child's primary need is to have secure, reliable connections with their caregivers, along with consistent, caring interactions. When these needs are not met, it can shake the very foundation of their emotional development.

Every experience that overwhelms your ability to cope - whether it is a one-time event or an ongoing situation - has the potential to create an emotional wound. These wounds are not about being weak or oversensitive. They are natural responses to situations where you perceive that your basic needs are not being met, and your brain did its best to protect you by creating meaning from these experiences.

Understanding this connection between your core needs and the meaning you give to painful experiences is crucial. It helps to explain why certain situations trigger such strong emotional responses, and why similar events might affect different people in different ways. Most importantly, it is the first step toward healing these deeper wounds and releasing the emotional baggage you have been carrying.

The Protection System

When these painful meanings and beliefs take hold, your brain's protection system kicks in. This is part of your survival instinct, and its job is simple: avoid pain at all costs. Think of it like an overprotective parent - it means well, but often oversteps its bounds. It might tell you never to trust anyone again, build emotional walls, or keep you from trying new things. While this system believes it is keeping you safe from future hurt, in reality, it is just adding more weight to your emotional baggage by reinforcing those painful beliefs about yourself and the world.

The primary purpose of this system is to shield you from anything it perceives as a threat to your emotional well-being. It is on alert and always ready to defend you against potential harm. However, it is essential to recognise that this system operates based on past experiences, which means it may perceive danger where none exists in your current life.

Imagine your inner world as a vast forest, where your emotions take the form of gentle Deer moving through meadows and hidden groves. These Deer represent your emotional self - naturally sensitive, attuned, and responsive to everything around them. With their wide eyes and acute senses, they perceive the subtle shifts in your experiences, embodying your capacity to feel deeply and authentically.

When they are emotionally unwounded, these Deer move freely through your inner landscape, expressing the full range of your feelings - from the joyful leaping through sunlit clearings to the quiet stillness of sadness in sheltered hollows. Your emotional self is vital to your human experience, as it connects you to others and lends meaning to your life.

But when painful experiences occur, these sensitive creatures become wounded. Your emotional wounds are like injured Deer - vulnerable beings who instinctively hide away for safety when hurt. Because we are wired to avoid pain at all costs, one of the first things your protection system does is encourage these wounded Deer to retreat into the deepest, darkest parts of your inner forest - what we call your subconscious mind.

There, hidden away from your everyday awareness, these emotionally wounded parts of yourself try to stay safe from further harm. Just as a wounded Deer will limp to a secluded thicket, your emotional wounds seek shelter where they will not be disturbed - buried beneath layers of busyness, numbness, or denial.

But just as a physical wound does not heal simply because you cannot see it, these emotional wounds - these wounded Deer - remain tender and hurting, even when they are out of sight. They need your attention, care, and gentle reassurance to truly heal. We will explore how to provide this healing attention in a later chapter, but for now, it is essential to understand that burying pain does not make it disappear - it simply pushes it into the shadows of your mind.

Your brain, witnessing these wounds, does what any protective force would do - it calls on guardians to keep these vulnerable Deer safe. Think of these guardians as two powerful protectors: a vigilant Wolf and a mighty Bear. While both share the mission of keeping your wounded Deer safe, they approach their protective duties differently.

The Wolf is your Preventor

The Wolf focuses on preventing any harm from reaching your vulnerable parts by:

- patrolling the forest borders, constantly scanning for danger
- creating careful rules and boundaries to keep threats at bay
- planning safe pathways through the forest
- trying to maintain strict control over who enters your inner world

- keeping the Deer hidden in safe havens, away from potential harm

The Bear is your Defender

When threats do break through the Wolf's careful defences, a different guardian springs into action - a mighty Bear who reacts with primal force.

This Bear:

- charges in when pain or danger is already present
- uses whatever means necessary to stop the hurt
- may react with overwhelming force
- focuses on immediate relief rather than long-term consequences
- can unintentionally cause damage in its desperate efforts to help

The Wolf and Bear are a Complete Protection System

In your inner forest, both your Wolf (prevention) and Bear (responder) guardians work together to create comprehensive protection through four distinct response patterns. Think of these not as isolated reactions, but as comprehensive protection strategies that incorporate both proactive and reactive elements.

The Fight Response: Protecting Through Power and Control

- Bear's Defensive Response: When threats break through despite these precautions, your Bear reacts with immediate shows of strength. This manifests as angry outbursts, harsh criticism, blame-shifting, or even rage blackouts, where you cannot remember what happened. Your Bear believes that pushing others away through aggression will keep your wounded parts safe from further harm.
- Wolf's Prevention Strategy: Your Wolf builds systems of control through criticism and high standards. It establishes rigid rules about how you and others should behave, creating environments where you feel powerful rather than vulnerable. You might develop beliefs like 'I must be stronger than everyone else' or 'The best defence is attack.' This guardian proactively scans for signs of disrespect or challenge, maintaining a critical eye to prevent anyone from gaining power over you.

Together, these create the Fight response pattern that you might recognise as:

- being quick to anger or criticism
- struggling to control impulses when triggered
- becoming highly defensive when feeling vulnerable
- using intimidation or bullying as a protective strategy
- finding it difficult to show softness or vulnerability

The Flight Response: Protecting Through Busyness and Escape

- Bear's Defensive Response: When painful emotions still break through, your Bear creates immediate escape routes. This might look like abruptly ending relationships, quitting jobs without notice, or using substances to numb feelings. Your Bear believes that fleeing from discomfort is the only way to survive overwhelming emotions.
- Wolf's Prevention Strategy: Your Wolf creates elaborate systems to avoid stillness and vulnerability. It fills your calendar with commitments, develops complex planning routines, and micromanages details to maintain a constant flow of activity. Through busyness and achievement, it tries to outrun emotional pain. Your Wolf believes that if you keep moving fast enough, the pain will never catch up to you.

Together, these create the Flight response pattern that you might recognise as:

- feeling anxious or panicked when not busy
- struggling to relax or be still
- using work or achievement as a distraction from feelings
- ending relationships when they become emotionally demanding
- feeling trapped by commitments or expectations

The Freeze Response: Protecting Through Disconnection

- Bear's Defensive Response: When painful emotions arise, your Bear responds by shutting down completely. This manifests as feeling numb, dissociating from your body, or becoming unable to make even small decisions. Your Bear believes that if you become completely still and invisible, the threat will pass you by.
- Wolf's Prevention Strategy: Your Wolf creates systems of isolation and emotional numbing to prevent pain. It

establishes routines of withdrawal, carefully limiting your exposure to potential hurt through social media scrolling, excessive TV watching, or other passive activities. Your Wolf builds beliefs like 'Life is pointless anyway' to protect you from disappointment.

Together, these create the Freeze response pattern that you might recognise as:

- feeling emotionally numb or disconnected
- struggling with procrastination and decision-making
- withdrawing from the world and social connections
- using passive distractions to avoid facing difficulties
- feeling confused about what is real or important

The Appease Response: Protecting Through Self-Sacrifice

Your protection system's Appease response develops as a sophisticated survival strategy when you have learned that your safety and belonging depend on keeping others happy. This protective pattern operates on two levels:

- Bear's Defensive Response: When your vigilance fails and conflict or disapproval emerges, your Bear immediately abandons your wants and needs in order to please others. This appears as agreeing when you disagree, apologising when you have done nothing wrong, or prioritising others' comfort over your own well-being. Your Bear shapes itself to meet others' expectations, believing that becoming whatever others want is the only way to stay safe.
- Wolf's Prevention Strategy: Your Wolf becomes hypervigilant about others' emotional states, developing an advanced system for monitoring facial expressions, tone of voice, and body language. It creates core beliefs like 'My worth depends on being helpful' and 'If I am not useful, I will be abandoned.' Your Wolf constantly scans for the slightest hint of disappointment or displeasure, always planning how to maintain approval through self-sacrifice and anticipating others' needs before they even express them.

Together, these create the Appease response pattern that you might recognise in your life as:

- difficulty saying 'no' or setting boundaries
- feeling responsible for others' emotions

- losing touch with your own needs and desires
- avoiding conflict at all costs
- constantly monitoring others' reactions and adjusting your behaviour accordingly
- experiencing underlying resentment despite your continued people-pleasing

This protective strategy may have helped you survive difficult relationships or environments in the past, but now it keeps you trapped in a cycle of self-abandonment. Your true self gets lost as you shape yourself to meet the real or perceived expectations of others, sacrificing your own truth to maintain approval and prevent rejection.

--

Understanding that each trauma response involves both proactive Wolf strategies and reactive Bear responses provides a more comprehensive map of your inner protection system. Most people develop a couple of primary response patterns, but might shift between different patterns depending on the situation, the relationship, or the type of threat they perceive.

The key insight is that both your Wolf and Bear are working together, using the same basic protection strategies with different timing and intensity. Neither is wrong for trying to protect you—they developed these patterns because, at some point in your life, they helped you survive difficult circumstances.

All Parts of Your Inner World

But your inner world is far more complex than just these protective responses. As mentioned earlier, imagine your psyche as a vast forest ecosystem, where different parts of you coexist. Throughout the forest, the gentle *Deer* represent your emotions - some roam healthy and free, while others still carry wounds from past hurts.

And flying between the trees, you will find a clever *Raven* - the embodiment of your analytical mind. This intelligent bird is constantly in motion, swooping through the forest, collecting shiny bits of information, and trying to make sense of everything it sees. The Raven represents your thinking self - that part of you that analyses, plans, questions, and attempts to understand your world.

Ravens are known for their remarkable problem-solving

abilities and adaptability. Your Raven mind excels at creating stories and explanations about everything, including your emotional wounds and the people who protect you. It is constantly chattering, offering a running commentary. Sometimes this analysis is helpful, providing insights that lead to healing. But at other times, the Raven can get caught in endless loops of overthinking, ruminating on painful memories, or creating worst-case scenarios about the future.

The Raven works through patterns and meanings. It perches on high branches, observing your life, including watching the Wolf's patrolling and the Bear's reactions. It is always trying to create a cohesive story about the meaning of events, why you feel what you feel, and why you do what you do. The Raven might tell you stories like 'I'm this way because of my childhood' or 'I always mess up relationships because I am broken.'

The Raven's constant noise - its croaks, rattles, and calls - mirrors your mind's endless internal chatter. Just as you might find it difficult to quiet your thoughts at night, the Raven rarely falls silent. It is always alert, analysing situations, reviewing past events, and making plans.

Watching on is a wise *Owl* representing your soul and its deep wisdom and guidance. The Owl understands that while the Wolf, Bear, and Raven all mean well, their protective instincts and analytical narratives can sometimes do more harm than good. The Owl sees how the Wolf's rigid control might prevent you from experiencing life fully, how the Bear's reactive responses might create new problems while trying to solve old ones, and how the Raven's endless analysis might keep you stuck in old stories rather than experiencing the present moment.

When trauma happens, especially in childhood, these aspects of yourself learn their roles. The Wolf becomes hypervigilant, determined never to let harm reach the Deer again. The Bear becomes ready to fight, run away from, or shut down from, or placate any pain that breaks through. The Raven develops complex theories and narratives about why the pain happened and projects into the future. Meanwhile, the wounded Deer retreat deeper into the shadows, carrying your unhealed emotional pain. While these responses may have been necessary for survival at the time, they might now be preventing you from healing and growing.

As we will get to in a later chapter in Part 3, a key to healing emotional wounds lies in helping the Wolf, Bear, and Raven to listen to and trust the Owl's wisdom. When they feel heard and honoured for their protective work, they can begin to relax their extreme roles. The Wolf can learn that not everything is a threat, the Bear can find gentler ways to handle pain when it arises, and the Raven can quiet its constant analysis to make space for direct experience. As they settle into more balanced roles, the wounded Deer can finally emerge from hiding and receive the tender care they need to heal.

This is the delicate dance of healing - honouring all aspects of your inner world while helping them find new ways to protect you, all under the gentle guidance of your Owl's wisdom. Remember, the Wolf, Bear, and Raven all developed their habits out of deep love and dedication to keeping your Deer safe. With patience and compassion, they can learn to serve you in healthier ways, allowing your inner forest to become a place where emotional wounds can heal and your Deer can once again move freely, expressing the full range of your emotions with balance and authenticity.

The Downside of Your Protection System

While your Wolf and Bear guardians mean well, their protection strategies can sometimes do more harm than good. For example, when your Wolf is on guard, how can you truly connect with others? When your Bear is encouraging withdrawal, how can you pursue your dreams?

The very system designed to protect you can end up adding to your emotional baggage in ways you might not realise. It reinforces limiting beliefs about yourself and others, quietly convincing you that these beliefs are facts rather than interpretations. It creates patterns of defensive behaviour that push people away just when connection might help you heal. The protective walls you build keep pain out, but they also block joy, love, and opportunity from entering your life.

Meanwhile, the constant state of hypervigilance—always scanning for threats based on past hurts—silently drains your energy, leaving you exhausted. Perhaps most significantly, this protection system keeps you stuck in survival mode, focused on just getting by rather than allowing you to thrive and experience life's fullness truly. What once shielded you has now become the very thing holding you back.

The Benefit of Understanding Emotional Wounds and Your Protection System

Understanding both your emotional wounds and how your protection system works to guard them is like being given a map of your inner forest. This map does not just show you where you are now - it reveals the paths that led you here and helps you chart a course forward.

When you understand how emotional wounds form, you begin to see that your reactions and patterns make perfect sense. Those wounded Deer in your inner forest weren't hurt by accident - each wound has a story, a reason, a moment when your heart needed protection and found it through these instinctive guardians. Your Wolf and Bear protectors were not being overly dramatic or unnecessarily cautious - they were responding to what were perceived as real threats in the best way they knew how.

This understanding brings compassion for both your wounded parts and your guardians. Your Wolf and Bear guardians are not your enemies; they are loyal protectors that developed during difficult times. They deserve your gratitude for the help they have provided in your survival. Even when their methods seem harsh or limiting, they are acting out of deep devotion to keeping you safe.

Learning to recognise when your protection system is activated is equally powerful. Perhaps you've noticed your Wolf guardian becoming hypervigilant about upcoming social situations, trying to control every detail in advance to prevent rejection. Or perhaps you catch your Bear guardian either going on the attack or preparing to retreat into emotional hibernation when conflict arises. These moments of awareness are like spotting familiar tracks in your inner forest - they tell you which guardian is active and why.

With this awareness, you can pause when you feel triggered and ask yourself important questions that create an opportunity for a new response. 'Is this situation truly threatening, or am I seeing it through the lens of an old wound?' This simple reflection can help you distinguish between genuine danger and echoes from your past. You might wonder, 'Which of my Deer is feeling frightened right now?' - acknowledging the vulnerable part of you that is feeling exposed. Or perhaps ask yourself, 'Is my Wolf's need for control or my Bear's emergency response really helping in this moment?' These questions interrupt the automatic protective reactions that have become second nature, giving you the chance to choose a response that serves your present reality rather than defending against shadows from your past.

Understanding also means recognising when these protection strategies have outlived their usefulness. Just as you would not want to stay in a fortress forever, you do not need to let your protection system control your entire life. Your guardians might be fighting battles that ended long ago, defending against threats that no longer exist in your adult life.

This does not mean asking your guardians to abandon their posts - that would only make them more defensive. Instead, with awareness and gentle work, you can help them learn new ways to keep your wounded Deer safe while still allowing them - and you - to explore, connect, and grow.

Once you understand the layout of your inner forest - where the wounded Deer hide, which paths your guardians patrol, what triggers them into high alert - you can begin to create new trails. You can show your guardians that while some parts of the forest may still need their fierce protection, other parts are safe for your Deer to venture out and graze peacefully.

This understanding becomes your compass for healing, guiding you through the complex terrain of your emotional landscape. It helps you recognise when you are being triggered by old wounds rather than responding to what is actually happening in the present moment. You will begin to understand why your protection system responds the way it does—not because it is broken, but because it is trying to protect you in the only way it knows how. This awareness naturally fosters compassion for both your wounds and your protective responses, allowing you to thank these guardians for their service while gently showing them that different approaches may now be needed. As trust builds, you can begin to help these vigilant parts of yourself relax in situations that are actually safe, creating space for new ways of responding that better serve your present life and allow for more authentic connection, joy, and growth.

Remember, this understanding is not about judging yourself or your guardians for past patterns. It is about gaining the insight needed to help all parts of yourself - the wounded Deer, the vigilant Wolf, the protective Bear, and the analytical Raven - find new ways to exist together in your inner forest.

How Unresolved Emotional Baggage Can Create More of the Same

Your emotional baggage is not just about the past - it can actively shape your present and future. This is because your unresolved emotional wounds, in a sense, act as a radio signal that keeps broadcasting the same painful patterns into your life.

When you carry old hurts and limiting beliefs, you unconsciously attract situations that match them. If, deep down, you believe 'I'm not good enough,' you will continue to find yourself in situations that seem to confirm this belief. Your protection system, still on guard from past hurts, stays alert for similar threats. While it thinks it is keeping you safe, it is actually keeping you stuck.

For example, if you experienced betrayal in the past, you might:

- be overly suspicious in new relationships
- push people away before they can get too close
- find yourself drawn to untrustworthy people
- see signs of betrayal even where none exist

This can create a self-fulfilling cycle. Your past wounds shape how you think, feel and act, which then creates experiences that reinforce those same wounds. It is like watching the same TV show over and over, just with different actors.

But you can break this cycle. By recognising your emotional baggage and learning to release it, you can start attracting experiences that match who you truly are, not who your wounds have trained you to be. Later in this book, you will learn specific techniques for letting go of this baggage and creating new, healthier patterns in your life.

But for now, the first step is simply becoming aware of these patterns. Notice when you are reacting from old wounds rather than responding to what is actually happening in the present moment. This awareness alone begins to weaken the grip of your emotional baggage.

--

As you have discovered throughout this chapter, emotional baggage is not just something you carry - it is a complex system of protection, wounding, and survival that involves every part of your inner world. You have met your protective Wolf and

Bear, your analytical Raven mind, your wounded Deer emotions, and glimpsed the wise Owl of your soul watching over it all.

Understanding these parts of yourself is the first step, but you might be wondering: 'Now what? How do I actually heal these wounds I have been carrying for so long?' That is exactly what awaits you in the corresponding chapter in Part 3 of this book. There, you will discover specific, practical methods for finally healing your emotional wounds. You will learn how to access your inner Owl's wisdom and use it to guide your entire system toward wholeness. The journey from understanding to healing is profound, and you are ready to take that next step.

WE MISUNDERSTAND WHAT LOVE REALLY IS

From the moment you are born, you are taught a skewed version of love. You learn that it is something you have to earn, that it is conditional on your behaviour, achievements, or appearance. TV, songs, and stories reinforce this idea, portraying love as something to be won or deserved. But what if we have been looking at love all wrong?

We Have Been Taught the Mind-Based Version of Love

How was love modelled for you growing up? Perhaps your parents gave you extra attention when you got good results at school, or maybe they withdrew their affection when you misbehaved. These early experiences teach us that love is transactional—something we receive when we are 'good' and lose when we are 'bad.' This conditional version of love follows us into adulthood. You might find yourself working overtime to please a partner, changing your appearance to be more attractive, or hiding parts of yourself that you fear might be rejected. You start to believe that love is something you must constantly work for and earn.

Consider your own experiences with love. Have you ever felt like you needed to change yourself to be loved? Or that you would be complete if you just found 'the one'? These are signs that you have bought into the mind-based version of love. And you are not alone.

Our culture bombards us with distorted messages about love: 'If they really loved you, they would know what you want without asking.' 'Love means never having to say you are sorry.' 'Love conquers all' These romantic notions sound lovely but set us up for disappointment. They make us think that love should be effortless, mind-reading, and powerful enough to solve all our problems.

Social media adds another layer of confusion with its highlight reels of picture-perfect relationships. You see the romantic proposals, the beautiful weddings, the holiday photos—but rarely the disagreements, the compromises, or the daily work of maintaining a healthy relationship. Films and books often portray love as a rollercoaster of intense emotions—the more dramatic, the more 'real' the love must be. But in truth, healthy love feels more like a safe harbour than a storm. It is consistent, reliable, and nurturing rather than wildly passionate, chaotic and all-consuming.

So, what we typically experience as love is mind-based love. It comes from our thoughts, conditioning and ego. It is calculated, measured, and always asking, 'What is in it for me?'

This mind-based love is often characterised by:

- Neediness and attachment - 'I can't live without you'.
- Fear of abandonment - 'What if they leave me?'.
- Possessiveness and jealousy - 'You are mine and no one else's'.
- Conditions - 'I'll love you if you make me happy'.
- The belief that someone else will 'complete' you - 'You're my missing piece'.

When you operate from a mind-based love, you are constantly on high alert. The undercurrent is fear, which is why you are scanning for threats to the relationship, keeping score of who did what for whom, and feeling insecure when your partner does not respond the way you want. This kind of love is exhausting because it requires constant validation and reassurance.

This misunderstanding of love does not just affect our relationships with others - it profoundly shapes our relationship with ourselves. The same conditional, transactional approach to love that we apply to others becomes the blueprint for how we treat ourselves. How often do you only feel worthy of your own approval when you have accomplished something impressive or look your best? This mind-based approach to self-love creates the same patterns of insecurity, measurement, and constant striving that plague our external relationships.

Self-love is not just a buzzword or a trendy concept. It is not about being narcissistic or selfish. It is about accepting yourself, flaws and all, and treating yourself with the same kindness and respect you would offer to someone you care about deeply. If you don't love yourself, how can you expect others to love you? How can you set healthy boundaries or confidently pursue your dreams? Without self-love, everything in life becomes more challenging.

When you lack true self-love, you might find yourself constantly replaying past mistakes in your mind, beating yourself up over and over. You might seek approval from others as if their opinion matters more than your own. You may let people walk all over you because deep down, you don't think you deserve better. Often, you put everyone else's needs before your own, leaving you drained and resentful. You might stay in situations that no longer serve you simply because you do not believe you deserve better.

The Problem with Romantic Love

The concept of romantic love as we know it today is relatively new in human history. It emerged in the Western world around the 12th century and has gradually evolved into what we now call 'falling in love'—that intoxicating rush of emotions and attraction. While these feelings are wonderful, they are often mistaken for love itself. The butterflies, the obsessive thinking about the other person, the feeling of being 'complete' when you are together—these are primarily biological and psychological responses, not love in its purest form.

Romantic love sweeps us up in a whirlwind of intense physical attraction, where we idealise our partner and see them through rose-coloured glasses. You might feel a powerful sense of destiny, as if the universe conspired to bring you together, while your thoughts become increasingly preoccupied with the relationship. This experience typically brings dramatic emotional highs when you are together and corresponding lows when you are apart—a rollercoaster of feelings that society has taught us represents 'true love' even though these intense sensations are actually temporary by nature.

These feelings are real and powerful, but temporary. When they inevitably fade (usually within six months to two years), many people conclude that they have 'fallen out of love' and move on to chase that high with someone new. But what if these feelings were just the doorway to something deeper? What if real love is something different?

One of the most common misconceptions about love is confusing it with attachment. While they often occur together, they are fundamentally different: Attachment is rooted in fear and need. It says, 'I need you to feel complete.' It creates dependency and anxiety about loss. When we are attached, we are concerned with what we can get from the relationship. Love, on the other hand, is giving rather than taking. It says, 'I want what is best for you, even if that doesn't include me.' Real love does not create dependency. It fosters growth and freedom.

This distinction is crucial because many relationships are built on mutual attachment rather than love. We feel an emotional high when we are with the person, and withdrawal when we are apart. We worry about losing them and feel threatened when they connect with others. This is not love—it is attachment masked as love. This same pattern plays out in our relationship with ourselves. Many of us are attached to certain self-images rather than truly loving ourselves. We are often attached to being seen as successful, attractive, or well-groomed. We fear losing these identities because we have linked our worth to them. True self-love, however, remains constant regardless of external achievements or appearances.

Another way we misunderstand love is by treating it as something that can be measured, quantified, or placed on a scale. We ask questions like: 'Do you love me more than yesterday?' 'How much do you love me?' 'Do you love me more than you love them?' These questions reveal our fundamental misunderstanding of what love actually is. Love is not something that increases or decreases day by day. It is not something that can be divided up like a pie, with less for one person if you give more to another.

This misunderstanding leads to constant insecurity and comparison in relationships. We often wonder where we stand, whether we are loved 'enough,' or if someone else is receiving more love than we are. We apply the same measurements to our self-worth. We measure our value based on external validation and achievements. We wonder if we are 'good enough' compared to others. We track our progress against arbitrary standards set by society. This measuring approach to self-love leaves us feeling perpetually inadequate, always striving but never quite arriving at a place of true self-acceptance.

From fairy tales to romantic comedies, our culture perpetuates the myth that there is one perfect person out there for each of us—our soulmate or 'the one.' This belief creates enormous pressure to find this mythical perfect match, and deep disappointment when real relationships fail to live up to this impossible standard. The truth is that many people could potentially be wonderful partners for us. There isn't just one person who can make us happy. Furthermore, no single relationship—no matter how wonderful—can fulfil all our needs for connection, growth, and love.

When we buy into the myth of 'the one,' we set ourselves up for disappointment. We expect our partner to be everything to us—lover, best friend, therapist, co-parent, financial partner, and more. No single relationship can bear the weight of all these expectations.

In our consumer-driven society, we have begun to treat love as a commodity—something to be traded, purchased, or acquired. We 'invest' in relationships expecting a 'return.' We think about what we are 'getting' out of a connection. We worry about whether we are getting a 'good deal' in our relationships. This transactional approach to love transforms something sacred into something commercial. It reduces the profound mystery of human connection to a cost-benefit analysis. When we view love through this lens, we are always calculating, always comparing, always wondering if we could get a better 'deal' elsewhere.

We treat self-love the same way – as something to be earned rather than our birthright. We believe we have to accomplish certain things or look a certain way to deserve our own approval. This commodification of self-love turns our relationship with ourselves into a constant negotiation: 'If I lose those ten pounds, then I will be worthy of love.' 'Once I get that promotion, then I will be good enough.' This approach keeps self-love perpetually out of reach, always contingent on the next achievement.

The Cost of Misunderstanding Love

When we neglect true self-love, the impacts can be profound and far-reaching. Most of us don't realise just how deep these effects go until they have already taken hold in our lives. The consequences build up gradually, often so slowly we don't notice until we are struggling under their weight.

The emotional toll can be devastating. Without true self-love, anxiety and depression can creep in. You might find yourself on an emotional rollercoaster, overreacting to small setbacks or feeling numb to life's joys. The inner critic grows louder, beating you up over every perceived mistake or flaw. Self-doubt becomes your constant companion, and decision-making feels increasingly difficult.

Many people describe feeling as though they are running on empty, going through the motions of life without any genuine sense of joy or purpose. Our relationships suffer too. When we don't value ourselves, we often accept treatment from others that mirrors our own lack of self-worth. This might mean staying in toxic relationships, struggling to say no, or becoming a people pleaser who prioritises everyone else's needs over their own. You might find yourself attracted to people who reinforce your negative self-image. Over time, resentment builds toward others for taking so much and toward yourself for allowing it.

Recognising these misunderstandings about love is the first step toward experiencing something more authentic and fulfilling. By becoming aware of the ways we have been misled about love—by our upbringing, our culture, and our own fears—we can begin to open ourselves to a different experience.

In the later chapter in Part 3 corresponding to this one, we will explore what real, heart-based love looks like and how we can begin to cultivate it in our lives. But for now, simply notice how these misunderstandings might be showing up in your own experience of love. Are you confusing love with attachment? Are you measuring and quantifying something that can't be measured? Are you treating love as a transaction rather than a gift? Do you extend the same kindness to yourself that you offer others?

By becoming aware of these patterns, you are already beginning to free yourself from them. You are taking the first step toward a more authentic understanding of love—one that is not based on what you have been taught, but on what you can experience when you open your heart beyond these limiting beliefs.

Understanding real love begins with recognising that the same principles apply whether we are loving others or ourselves. When we begin to grasp what love really is – unconditional, non-transactional, and rooted in genuine care rather than fear – we transform not just our relationships with others, but the fundamental relationship we have with ourselves. And that might be the most important relationship of all.

Now that we have uncovered how we misunderstand love - confusing it with need, control, or validation - you might be asking, 'So what does real love actually look like?' That is exactly what we will explore in the corresponding chapter in Part 3. There, you will discover how to cultivate authentic love that flows from wholeness rather than emptiness, and create relationships built on genuine connection rather than old wounds. Recognising what is not love is the first step to finding what is.

LACK OF SELF-CARE

Imagine for a moment that you are your own best friend. How would you treat yourself? Would you be kind, patient, and understanding? Or would you be harsh, critical, and unforgiving? How you answer these questions can reveal a great deal about your relationship with yourself. And that relationship shapes every aspect of your life.

Self-care is the practical expression of self-love. It means prioritising your wellbeing through basic acts, such as getting enough sleep, eating nourishing food, and staying active. It involves making time for activities that bring you joy, setting clear boundaries with others, and seeking support when needed. Self-care encompasses creating space for solitude and reflection, maintaining your physical and mental well-being, and learning to say 'no' to things that drain your energy. Yet despite knowing its importance, we are facing a self-care crisis. Many of us are running on empty, giving from depleted reserves, and wondering why we feel so exhausted and disconnected. This is not just a personal problem—it is a cultural one.

Our society often glorifies busyness and sacrifice, especially for women and caregivers. People are taught that putting ourselves last is virtuous, that pushing through exhaustion is admirable, and that asking for help is a sign of weakness. Social media adds another layer of complexity, turning self-care into performative acts rather than genuine nurturing. The result? Millions of people are ignoring their basic needs while wondering why they feel so terrible.

True self-care encompasses five interconnected dimensions of our being, and neglecting any one of them can throw the whole system out of balance:

Physical Neglect

The physical dimension is perhaps the most obvious area of self-care, yet many of us consistently override our body's basic needs:

- Sleep deprivation: Cutting sleep short to fit more into your day, exposing yourself to blue light before bed, or using substances like alcohol that disrupt sleep quality.
- Poor nutrition: Skipping meals, eating primarily processed foods, not staying hydrated, or using food to

numb emotions rather than nourish your body.
- Movement deficiency: Sitting for hours without breaks, avoiding physical activity, or alternatively, pushing your body too hard without adequate recovery.
- Ignoring body signals: Pushing through pain, fatigue, or illness; treating your body like a machine that should function without maintenance.

Your body is designed to send you clear signals about what it needs, but years of ignoring these signals can disconnect you from this innate wisdom. Many people reach the point where they only notice their body's needs when they have reached a crisis point—extreme fatigue, illness, or pain that can no longer be ignored.

Emotional Neglect

Emotional self-care involves acknowledging, accepting, and expressing your feelings in healthy ways. When this dimension is neglected, you might:

- Suppress emotions: Pushing feelings down, telling yourself you 'shouldn't' feel a certain way, or using distraction to avoid uncomfortable emotions.
- Lack emotional awareness: Being disconnected from your feelings until they erupt in outbursts or manifest as physical symptoms.
- Engage in emotional self-harm: Harsh self-criticism, rumination on past mistakes, or comparisons to others that leave you feeling inadequate.
- Avoid emotional processing: Never creating space to work through difficult experiences, leading to accumulated emotional baggage.

Without healthy emotional self-care, feelings get stuck rather than flowing naturally through you. This creates an emotional backlog that can manifest as anxiety, depression, irritability, or emotional numbness.

Mental Neglect

Your mind needs both stimulation and rest. Mental self-care involves tending to your cognitive needs and maintaining a healthy thought life. Signs of mental neglect include:

- Information overload: Constant consumption of news, social media, and content without breaks for integration.

- Negative thought patterns: Allowing pessimistic, catastrophic, or self-defeating thoughts to dominate your mental landscape.
- Mental stagnation: Lack of learning, curiosity, or exposure to new ideas and perspectives.
- Cognitive overwhelm: Trying to keep everything in your head rather than using systems to organise information and tasks.

Your mind, like any ecosystem, needs tending. Without intentional care, it can become either an overgrown jungle of tangled thoughts or a barren landscape lacking creativity and insight.

Social Neglect

Humans are inherently social beings, yet many of us neglect our need for meaningful connection:

- Isolation: Withdrawing from relationships due to busyness, exhaustion, or past hurts.
- Superficial connections: Maintaining shallow relationships without the depth and genuineness that truly nourish us.
- People-pleasing: Saying yes when you want to say no, hiding your true self to be accepted, or prioritising others' needs at a high cost to yourself.
- Toxic relationships: Remaining in connections that consistently diminish rather than enhance your wellbeing.

The quality of your relationships has a profound impact on your health and happiness. Social neglect can leave you feeling lonely even when surrounded by people, because the essential ingredients of true connection—vulnerability, authenticity, and mutual care—are missing.

Spiritual Neglect

The spiritual dimension concerns your connection to something larger than yourself and your sense of meaning and purpose. This does not necessarily involve religion, though it can. Spiritual neglect might look like:

- Disconnection from meaning: Going through the motions of life without a sense of purpose or larger significance.
- Value incongruence: Living in ways that conflict with your core values, creating internal dissonance.

- Nature deprivation: Lack of time in natural settings that remind you of your place in the larger web of life.
- Absence of contemplative practices: No space for reflection, wonder, gratitude, or connection to something beyond the material world.

Spiritual self-care grounds you in what matters most. Without it, you can achieve external success while feeling internally empty, wondering, 'Is this all there is?'

When we neglect self-care, the impacts can be profound and far-reaching. Most of us don't realise just how deep these effects go until they have already taken hold in our lives. The consequences build up gradually, often so slowly we don't notice until we are struggling under their weight.

Remember what happens to a car when it's never serviced. Eventually, things start to break down. The same happens with us. When we consistently put ourselves last, ignore our body's signals, or push through exhaustion, our system begins to falter.

Physical Impact

Physical symptoms often show up first:

- persistent fatigue that sleep does not resolve
- frequent illnesses as your immune system weakens
- headaches, backaches, and other pain signals
- digestive issues like bloating, constipation, or IBS
- disrupted sleep patterns despite feeling exhausted
- unexplained weight changes as your body struggles to maintain balance
- skin problems, hair loss, or other visible signs of internal stress
- hormonal imbalances affecting everything from mood to metabolism

These symptoms are not just inconveniences—they are your body's increasingly urgent attempts to get your attention. Ignoring them only forces your body to 'speak' louder through more severe symptoms.

Emotional Impact

The emotional toll can be even more devastating:

- anxiety that ranges from background worry to full-

blown panic
- depression or persistent low mood
- emotional numbness or disconnection
- irritability and a shortened fuse
- feeling overwhelmed by relatively minor challenges
- reduced resilience when facing life's inevitable setbacks
- stronger emotional reactions that seem disproportionate
- difficulty experiencing joy, even in previously pleasurable activities

Without self-care, your emotional regulation system begins to malfunction. You may find yourself switching between intense reactions and emotional flatness, struggling to find a balanced middle ground.

Mental Impact

Your cognitive function suffers too:

- brain fog and difficulty concentrating
- memory problems and forgetfulness
- reduced creativity and problem-solving ability
- negative thought spirals that are hard to break
- indecisiveness or difficulty making even simple choices
- rumination on past mistakes or future worries
- diminished ability to learn new information
- mental exhaustion after tasks that once felt easy

Your brain is an organ that requires proper care to function optimally. Without it, your mental clarity, sharpness, and flexibility all decline.

Social Impact

Our relationships suffer, too. When we don't value ourselves, we often accept treatment from others that mirrors our own lack of self-worth. This might mean:

- staying in toxic relationships that are draining
- struggling to set or maintain boundaries
- becoming a people-pleaser who puts everyone else's needs first
- attracting partners who reinforce a negative self-image
- withdrawing from connections due to lack of energy or fear of rejection
- developing resentment toward others for being 'takers'
- feeling chronically misunderstood or unsupported

- losing the capacity for genuine intimacy and vulnerability

Over time, these patterns create distance in your relationships. The connections become increasingly transactional rather than genuinely nurturing, leaving you feeling isolated even when surrounded by people.

Professional Impact

Your work life can take a hit as well:

- reduced productivity and efficiency
- difficulty focusing on tasks or prioritising effectively
- increased mistakes or oversights
- loss of passion or purpose in your work
- reluctance to pursue opportunities due to exhaustion or insecurity
- undervaluing your contributions and accepting less than you deserve
- taking on too much and struggling to delegate
- burnout that leaves you questioning your career path

Without healthy self-care, your professional life becomes a drain rather than a source of fulfilment, regardless of your natural talents or the inherent meaning in your work.

The Downward Spiral

Perhaps most insidiously, this neglect creates a downward spiral. The less we care for ourselves, the worse we feel. The worse we feel, the less worthy we feel of care and attention. And so the cycle continues, deepening with each rotation until we find ourselves thoroughly disconnected from our own needs, wants, and worth.

The effects ripple outward, too, touching everyone around us. When we are running on empty, we have less to give to others—less patience, less presence, less genuine connection. Our relationships become transactional rather than nurturing. We might even unconsciously teach others, especially our children, that self-neglect is normal or even virtuous.

Common Barriers to Self-Care

Understanding why you struggle with self-care is essential for breaking these patterns. Several common barriers prevent us from giving ourselves the care we deserve:

Conditioning and Upbringing

Many of us grew up in environments where self-care was neither modelled nor encouraged:

- parents who themselves never practised self-care
- messages that prioritising your needs is selfish or indulgent
- cultural or religious teachings that extol the virtues of sacrifice and suffering
- family systems where expressing needs is discouraged or punished

These early messages become deeply internalised, creating unconscious resistance to self-care even when we know it is essential.

Mistaken Beliefs About Self-Care

Our understanding of what constitutes self-care may be distorted:

- equating self-care with expensive indulgences or 'treating yourself'
- believing it requires large amounts of time you don't have
- viewing it as an all-or-nothing proposition rather than small daily choices
- confusing self-care with self-improvement
- thinking of it as a reward for hard work rather than a fundamental need

These misconceptions make genuine self-care seem either trivial or unattainable, rather than recognising it as the essential foundation it is.

The Busyness Trap

Our modern culture often equates busyness with importance and worth:

- overloaded schedules that leave no margin for rest or reflection
- digital connectivity that blurs boundaries between work and personal time

- social media that creates pressure to be productive, successful, and exciting
- economic pressures that necessitate overwork for many
- comparison with others who seem to 'do it all' effortlessly

In this context, slowing down for self-care can trigger a fear of falling behind or not meeting societal expectations.

The Caregiver Identity

Many people, especially women, derive their sense of worth from caring for others:

- building an identity around being needed by others
- feeling guilty when taking time for yourself
- believing that self-sacrifice proves your love and commitment
- discomfort with receiving rather than giving care
- fear that prioritising yourself will lead to abandonment or rejection

When your value is tied to what you do for others, self-care can feel not just uncomfortable but almost threatening to your sense of self.

Past Trauma and Unworthiness

Deeper wounds may create fundamental barriers to self-care:

- believing at your core that you don't deserve care and attention
- early experiences that taught you your needs do not matter
- associating care and attention with manipulation or danger
- using self-neglect as a form of self-punishment for perceived inadequacy
- unconscious belief that suffering somehow makes you worthy or virtuous

Understanding how deeply this neglect affects us can be the wake-up call we need to start treating ourselves with greater care and respect. The good news is that the self-neglect cycle can be broken at any point. Small shifts in how you care for yourself can create positive upward spirals that gradually transform your relationship with yourself and, by extension, every other aspect of your life.

The Connection Between Self-Care and Your Health

There is a profound truth that ancient wisdom has long understood and modern science is now confirming: your emotional well-being and physical health are intimately connected. When you carry emotional baggage, live with chronic stress, or neglect your self-care, your body keeps score—and eventually, it will present you with the bill.

The word 'disease' literally means 'dis-ease'—a lack of ease in the body, mind, or spirit. When you are constantly stressed, suppressing emotions, or running on empty from poor self-care, you are living in a state of dis-ease. Your nervous system remains on high alert, your immune system becomes compromised, and your body's natural healing mechanisms are disrupted.

Think about how you feel physically when you are:

- carrying unresolved anger or resentment
- constantly worrying about the future
- suppressing grief or sadness
- living with chronic guilt or shame
- feeling overwhelmed and unsupported

Your body responds to these emotional states with tension, inflammation, digestive issues, sleep problems, headaches, and a host of other symptoms. This is not weakness—it is your body's way of communicating that something needs attention.

When you don't take care of yourself or fully process emotional wounds, your body holds onto everything. Trauma researcher Dr Bessel van der Kolk demonstrates that these experiences can literally reshape our bodies and brains.

Your body stores it all:

- the betrayal that made you guard your heart
- the criticism that made you shrink
- the abandonment that made you overly self-reliant
- years of overwhelming stress you have been carrying

These memories live in your muscles, nervous system, and organs. They create patterns of tension and inflammation that can manifest as chronic pain, digestive issues, or even autoimmune conditions. Your body keeps the score of every unprocessed hurt and every moment you put yourself last.

In Part 3 of this book, we will explore practical ways to build a comprehensive self-care practice that addresses all five dimensions we have discussed. You will learn specific strategies for listening to your body's wisdom, processing emotions healthily, tending to your mental well-being, cultivating nourishing relationships, and connecting with a deeper meaning and purpose.

For now, simply notice. Notice when you override your body's signals for rest or nourishment. Notice when you dismiss your emotions or neglect your need for connection. Notice the messages and beliefs that keep you locked in patterns of self-neglect.

And perhaps most importantly, notice with compassion rather than judgment. The patterns you have developed didn't form overnight, and they won't change overnight either. But with consistent small steps towards greater self-care, you can gradually transform your relationship with yourself and create a foundation for thriving in every area of your life.

Remember, you deserve care not because of what you accomplish or provide to others, but simply because you exist. Your inherent worth does not diminish when you rest, say no, or prioritise your wellbeing. In fact, it is only when you truly value yourself that you can offer your authentic gifts to the world from a place of fullness rather than depletion.

HANG UPS ABOUT MONEY

Do you ever feel like you are drowning in a sea of conflicting messages about money? From the moment you were old enough to understand what money is, you have probably been bombarded with contradictory advice. 'Money can't buy happiness,' they say solemnly, but then in the next breath, advertisements scream that you need the latest smartphone, designer clothes, or luxury car to feel complete. It is no wonder so many of us feel confused and anxious about our finances.

Think about all the mixed messages you have heard about money throughout your life:

- 'Money is the root of all evil,' but also 'You need money to make a difference in the world.'
- 'Live within your means,' but also 'Treat yourself, you deserve it.'
- 'Save for a rainy day,' but also 'You can't take it with you when you die.'

These contradictory messages don't just create confusion—they create real emotional turmoil. You may feel guilty when you spend money on yourself, anxious about your financial future, or ashamed if you don't have as much as your friends or colleagues. Money is not just currency. It has become intertwined with our self-worth, identity, sense of security and safety, and our place in society.

The Emotional Weight of Financial Stress

Financial stress is one of the heaviest burdens many of us carry. In fact, financial worries are consistently ranked among the top sources of stress for adults. This kind of stress does not just affect your bank account—it seeps into every area of your life. When you are worried about money, you might find yourself lying awake at night, your mind racing with thoughts about bills, debt, or financial uncertainty. You might notice tension in your relationships as you and your partner disagree about spending priorities. Your health might suffer as chronic stress takes its toll, leading to headaches, digestive issues, and a weakened immune system.

And perhaps most insidiously, financial stress can cut you off from joy and presence. When you are constantly worrying about money, it is hard to enjoy the moment you are in fully. A beautiful sunset becomes a brief distraction from your money worries rather than a moment of awe and gratitude.

Our Protection System and Money

Remember how we talked about our protection system in an earlier chapter? That internal mechanism that tries to keep us safe from emotional harm? Well, it has a lot to say about money, too.

If you experienced financial insecurity or scarcity as a child, your protection system might have developed strong beliefs about money to help you cope. Perhaps you learned that money is scarce and can disappear at any moment, so you need to hoard every penny. Or maybe you witnessed your parents fighting about money, so it decided that money equals conflict and is something to avoid thinking about. These protective beliefs might have helped you cope with difficult situations in the past, but now they are part of your emotional baggage, weighing you down and limiting your financial serenity.

Common Money Hang-Ups

Let us examine some of the most common financial concerns people have. As you read through these, notice if any of them resonate with you.

The Scarcity Mindset

Do you often feel like there is never enough money, even though your needs are objectively met? A scarcity mindset keeps you in a state of fear and anxiety about money. You might find yourself obsessively checking your bank account, feeling a pit in your stomach when you have to spend money, or being unable to enjoy what you have because you are worried about the future.

This mindset often stems from early experiences of financial insecurity or from growing up with parents who themselves had a scarcity mindset. Your safeguarding system learned that financial security is fragile, so it keeps you on high alert to protect you from potential loss.

Money Avoidance

Do you put off checking your bank balance, let bills pile up unopened, or feel a sense of dread whenever you need to make financial decisions? Money avoidance is a common response to financial anxiety. It may feel easier to avoid thinking about money than to face potential problems or difficult decisions.

This hang-up often develops when money has been associated with negative emotions, such as shame, conflict, or inadequacy. Your protection system tries to shield you from these painful feelings by encouraging you to avoid the topic altogether. Unfortunately, this often exacerbates financial problems in the long run.

The 'More Is Better' Trap

Have you ever thought, 'If I just had X amount more money, then I'd be happy'? The 'more is better' trap is the belief that greater wealth automatically leads to greater happiness and well-being. You might find yourself constantly chasing the next pay rise, the next investment opportunity, or the next level of financial success, believing that once you reach it, you will finally feel secure and content.

This hang-up is reinforced by our consumer culture, which constantly pushes the message that more is better. Your protection system might have latched onto this idea because it offers a simple solution to complex emotional needs—if you are feeling inadequate or insecure, just make more money.

Financial Comparison

Do you find yourself looking at friends' holiday photos on social media and wondering how they can afford such luxuries? Or maybe you feel a twinge of jealousy when a colleague mentions their new house or car? Financial comparison is when you measure your own financial situation against others and usually find yourself coming up short.

In today's world of carefully curated social media personas, it is easier than ever to fall into the comparison trap. What you don't see is the debt, the family help, or the sacrifices that might be behind those enviable purchases. Your protection system uses comparison as a way to evaluate your status and safety, but in our complex modern world, these comparisons are rarely accurate or helpful.

Money Shame

Are you embarrassed about your financial situation? Perhaps you hide your spending from your partner, lie about the cost of things, or avoid financial conversations altogether because they make you feel inadequate or ashamed.

Money shame can stem from cultural or family messages about what financial success should look like. If you have internalised the belief that your worth as a person is tied to your financial success, then financial struggles can feel like personal failures rather than normal parts of life.

--

These hang-ups aren't just abstract psychological concepts—they have real, painful impacts on your life. They can lead to destructive financial behaviours like overspending to temporarily boost your mood or status, underspending and denying yourself basic comforts out of fear, taking on unsustainable debt to maintain appearances, avoiding important financial planning for the future, making fear-based investment decisions, staying in unfulfilling jobs just for the paycheque, and allowing money conflicts to damage your relationships.

More fundamentally, these hang-ups keep you disconnected from what truly matters. When your relationship with money is driven by fear, shame, or confusion, it is hard to use money as a tool to support your authentic values and purpose.

As we close this chapter, you might wonder how to actually move past these money blocks. That is what we will explore in Part 3, where you will discover practical strategies for achieving financial serenity - that peaceful, confident relationship with money where decisions come from wisdom, not fear. For now, celebrate the awareness you have gained. Understanding your money story is the first step to changing it.

NEGATIVE ENERGY DRAGS YOU DOWN

Have you ever left a conversation feeling completely exhausted, even though you barely moved a muscle? Perhaps it was a catch-up with a friend who always seems to be going through a crisis, or a meeting with a colleague who constantly complains. Your body feels heavy, your mind feels foggy, and all you want to do is take a nap, even though you weren't doing anything physically demanding. Or perhaps you have walked into certain places, such as your workplace, a relative's house, or even a shop, and immediately felt your energy plummet. Something about the environment just feels 'off,' even if you can't quite explain why.

These experiences are not just a figment of your imagination. What you are feeling is the very real effect of negative energy, and it affects your life in more ways than you might realise.

Your energy is like your phone battery. You start each day with a certain amount of charge, and different activities either drain or recharge that battery. Some people, places, and situations act like those power-hungry apps that drain your battery surprisingly quickly. Others are like having your phone connected to a faulty charger - you think you are recharging, but you are actually losing power.

The thing is that we often don't notice these energy drains until we are already running on empty. We push through the fatigue, blame it on lack of sleep or stress, and keep going. We might even feel guilty for being 'too sensitive' or 'making a big deal out of nothing' when certain interactions leave us feeling depleted.

Your energy is one of your most precious resources. It affects everything in your life: your health, your relationships, your work performance, your creativity, your decision-making ability, and even your capacity to create the life you want. When negative sources are consistently draining your energy, it is like trying to drive a car with the handbrake on. You can still move forward, but it requires significantly more effort than it should, and in the process, you are causing damage.

In this chapter, we are going to explore what is really happening when you experience these energy drains. You will learn why certain people, places, and situations leave you feeling depleted, how to recognise the signs of energy drain before you run on empty, and, most importantly, why protecting your energy is not selfish; it is essential.

Understanding Energy and Vibration

Everything in your life, including you, is made of energy. This is not just some mystical concept; it is a scientific fact. Every atom in your body, every thought in your mind, and every emotion you feel is a form of energy vibrating at a particular frequency. Like music: high vibrations are like uplifting melodies that make you want to dance, while low vibrations are like heavy beats that make you want to sink into your chair.

You are already familiar with energy and vibration, even if you don't realise it. Have you ever walked into a room right after an argument and felt the 'tension in the air,' even though nobody said a word? Or have you noticed how one person's genuine smile and enthusiasm can lift the mood of an entire group? That is energy at work.

Your personal energy field is like a radio signal that constantly broadcasts and receives. When you are feeling happy, confident, and full of life, you are vibrating at a high frequency. It's as if you are playing an uplifting song that attracts similar, positive energies. People are naturally drawn to you, opportunities seem to flow more easily, and life feels more effortless. But when you are stressed, fearful, or surrounded by negativity, your vibration drops. It is like switching from that uplifting song to a heavy, discordant tune. You might feel sluggish, irritable, or stuck. Problems seem bigger, solutions feel harder to find, and even simple tasks can feel overwhelming.

Your energy does not just affect how you feel. It influences every aspect of your life:

- Your Physical Health: Low Vibration energy can manifest as physical symptoms like fatigue, headaches, or a weakened immune system. When your energy is consistently low, your body has to work harder just to maintain basic functions.
- Your Mental Clarity: Have you noticed how much sharper your thinking is when you are feeling energised and positive? That is because high vibration energy supports clear thinking and creative problem-solving. When your energy is low, even simple decisions can feel confusing.
- Your Relationships: Energy is contagious. When your vibration is high, you naturally attract and maintain healthier relationships. However, when you are stuck in

low-vibration patterns, you may find yourself drawn to or tolerate relationships that further drain you.

- Your Success: Your energy directly affects your ability to act, persist through challenges, and recognise opportunities. High vibration energy helps you stay motivated and resilient, while low vibration energy can keep you stuck in patterns of procrastination and self-doubt.

Think of your energy like water in a glass. When the water is clear and fresh, it is life-giving and rejuvenating. But if the water becomes stagnant or contaminated, it cannot properly nourish you. In the same way, your energy needs to stay clear and flowing to support your wellbeing.

The good news is that you are not just a passive receiver of energy - you are also a creator and transmitter. Just as a cloudy glass of water can be filtered and refreshed, you can learn to clear negative energy and raise your vibration. But first, you need to understand what is draining your energy.

Common Energy Drains

Let us examine the various ways your energy can be depleted. Understanding these sources is like having a map of energy leaks in your life - once you can identify them, you can start addressing them.

People Who Drain Your Energy

Have you ever noticed how some people seem to leave you feeling exhausted after every interaction? These 'energy vampires' come in various forms:

- The Constant Complainer: Nothing is ever right in their world. Even good news gets a negative spin. After hearing their complaints, you feel weighed down and exhausted.
- The Drama Magnet: Their life is a constant series of crises. They pull you into their problems, making you feel responsible for fixing everything.
- The Guilt Tripper: They are masters at making you feel bad about setting boundaries or taking care of yourself. 'How could you be so selfish?' is their favourite phrase.
- The Chronic Taker: These relationships feel one-sided. They are there when they need something, but mysteriously absent when you need support.
- The Controller: They always know better than you do.

Their need to micromanage and criticise leaves you doubting yourself and feeling depleted.

Places and Environments

Your surroundings can have a surprising impact on your energy levels:

- Cluttered Spaces: When your environment is chaotic and disorganised, your energy gets scattered too. Each piece of clutter is like a small weight on your shoulders.
- Noisy Environments: Constant background noise, especially if you can't control it, can steadily drain your energy throughout the day.
- Artificial Environments: Spaces with poor air quality, harsh lighting, or no natural elements can leave you feeling depleted and disconnected.
- Places with Bad Memories: Locations associated with difficult experiences can trigger an automatic energy drop, even if the situation has long passed.

Situations and Circumstances

Certain situations can act like energy sinkholes:

- High-Pressure Deadlines: When you are constantly racing against the clock, your energy gets burned up by stress and anxiety.
- Financial Worries: Money concerns can create a constant background drain on your energy.
- Unresolved Conflicts: Ongoing tensions, whether at work or in relationships, steadily leak your energy even when you are not actively dealing with them.
- Information Overload: Constant news updates, endless emails, and social media can overwhelm your system and scatter your energy.

Habits and Behaviours

Sometimes, we are our own worst energy drains:

- Poor Sleep Patterns: Irregular sleep or not getting enough rest means you are starting each day with a partially charged battery.
- Unhealthy Eating: Processed foods, too much sugar, or irregular meals can create energy crashes and leave you feeling sluggish.

- Excessive Screen Time: Hours spent scrolling or binge-watching can leave you feeling oddly tired despite being physically inactive.
- Procrastination: Putting things off can create a nagging energy drain that grows the longer you avoid tasks.

Internal Sources

Often, the biggest energy drains come from within:

- Negative Self-Talk: That critical inner voice constantly pointing out your flaws and failures is like a slow leak in your energy tank.
- Unresolved Emotions: Suppressed anger, buried grief, or unacknowledged fear act like heavy weights on your energy system.
- Limiting Beliefs: Beliefs like 'I'm not good enough' or 'Things never work out for me' create resistance that drains your energy.
- Perfectionism: The need to get everything exactly right can exhaust you before you even start.
- Past Traumas: Unhealed wounds from the past can create ongoing energy drains that affect your present life.

Energy drains often work together. For example, a toxic relationship may lead to negative self-talk, which in turn affects your sleep, leaving you too tired to maintain healthy habits. It is like a domino effect of energy depletion.

The Hidden Impact

When your energy is constantly being drained, the effects go far beyond just feeling tired. Like a stone thrown into a pond, energy drains create ripples that touch every aspect of your life. Let's uncover these hidden impacts that you might not realise are connected to your depleted energy.

Physical Effects

Your body can often be the first place to show signs of energy drain:

- You might experience chronic fatigue as a deep exhaustion that sleep does not seem to fix, potentially leaving you dependent on caffeine just to complete basic daily tasks.

- Your immune system may weaken, making you more susceptible to illnesses during stressful periods.
- Some people develop mysterious aches and pains—headaches, back tension, or stomach issues—which can be your body storing negative energy as physical tension.
- Even when exhausted, you might face disrupted sleep, possibly tossing and turning all night or waking up feeling unrefreshed.
- Weight changes can occur when your body's natural balance is thrown off, whether through comfort eating or a loss of appetite.

These physical symptoms are not just inconveniences—they can be your body's way of signalling that something deeper needs attention.

Emotional Consequences

Your emotional landscape can take a hit when your energy is low:

- You might experience mood swings where small things that normally would not bother you suddenly feel overwhelming, potentially causing you to snap at loved ones or cry over minor frustrations.
- Anxiety may increase as your emotional resilience drops, possibly making everything feel more threatening and everyday stress harder to handle.
- For some people, emotional numbness can set in when energy is consistently drained, as if their emotional system has gone into power-saving mode.
- You might notice a loss of joy: activities that once brought pleasure now feel flat or meaningless, leaving you going through the motions without really engaging.

Mental Implications

Your mental clarity and cognitive function can suffer when your energy is low:

- Some people experience brain fog that makes simple decisions feel overwhelming, like standing in front of your wardrobe unable to choose what to wear.
- You might notice poor concentration, with you reading the same paragraph repeatedly and tasks taking much longer than usual.
- Creativity may diminish, possibly making problem-

solving harder and new ideas more difficult to generate.
- Memory issues can develop, potentially leading you to forget appointments, misplace things, or struggle to recall important details that once came easily to you.

Impact on Relationships

Energy drains can affect your connections with others:

- You might find yourself withdrawing as social situations become too demanding, perhaps even finding that answering a text message feels like too much effort.
- Relationship tension can build when a depleted state leaves you with less patience and emotional availability, sometimes turning minor irritations into bigger disagreements.
- Boundary issues can develop when low energy makes it harder to maintain healthy limits, potentially leading you to say 'yes' when you really need to say 'no.'
- Intimacy may decrease in connections with partners, friends, and family, as deep connection requires energy you might not have available, sometimes making relationships feel more superficial.

Career and Success Limitations

Your professional life can bear the brunt of energy depletion:

- You might notice decreased performance: once-manageable tasks now seem overwhelming, and your work quality may suffer despite putting in more hours.
- Opportunities may be missed as low energy could make you less likely to put yourself forward for new challenges or take calculated risks.
- Career progress can slow down, as advancing often requires energy for networking, learning new skills, or taking on extra responsibilities.
- Your earning potential might be affected through reduced productivity, missed opportunities, or difficulty pursuing additional income streams.
- If you are in a management position, leadership challenges can arise when depleted energy affects your whole team, potentially making it difficult to inspire others when you are feeling drained yourself.

The Cumulative Effect

Perhaps the most insidious aspect of energy drains is their tendency to compound over time. Each area might affect the others, potentially creating a downward spiral. Physical fatigue can lead to reduced physical activity, which may impact your mood and emotional well-being. Emotional exhaustion might strain your relationships, possibly increasing your overall stress levels. Mental fog can affect your work performance, potentially leading to financial concerns or uncertainty. Career stagnation can impact your self-esteem, potentially straining your personal relationships.

This cycle can feel overwhelming. But the good news is that just as negative energy creates a downward spiral, positive energy can create an upward one. Once you start addressing your energy drains, each slight improvement can build on the others. Understanding these hidden impacts is crucial because it helps you recognise the actual cost of allowing energy drains to continue unchecked.

Remember, you don't have to accept energy drain as usual. These impacts are not just 'the way things are'. They are signs that something must change. And change is possible when you know what to look for and how to address it.

Now that you understand how negative energy from people, places, and situations drains your vitality and dims your light, you might be asking, 'How do I protect myself and stay positive?' That is precisely what we will explore in the corresponding chapter in Part 3.

THE INNER MASCULINE AND FEMININE DIVIDE

We all carry both masculine and feminine qualities within us, regardless of our gender. Think of these attributes as complementary forces that, when balanced, create harmony in our lives and relationships. Yet many of us find ourselves disconnected from these aspects, often without realising it.

Each of your inner masculine and feminine attributes has its own essential characteristics. Feminine qualities tend to be receptive, passive, intuitive, and inward-focused, while masculine qualities are typically projective, active, expansive, and outward-focused. Neither is better than the other—they are designed to work together, like breathing in and breathing out.

When these attributes express themselves in their natural, healthy state, they bring incredible gifts to your life. Your natural feminine qualities manifest as:

- unconditional love and understanding
- nurturing tenderness and kindness
- intuitive creativity and sensitivity
- a capacity for stillness, flow, and surrender

Meanwhile, your natural masculine qualities show up as:

- confidence and inner strength
- responsibility and focus
- logical thinking and clarity
- protection, boundaries, and discipline

But like any aspect of ourselves, these attributes can become wounded. When your feminine side is hurt, it might express itself through victimhood, manipulation, neediness, or emotional instability. When your masculine side is damaged, it can emerge as dominance, aggression, criticism, or emotional unavailability.

Notice how these wounded expressions connect to the four protection responses we explored earlier. The wounded feminine typically triggers a freeze (shutting down emotionally) or an appease response (people-pleasing to avoid conflict). The wounded masculine usually activates fight (attacking or controlling) or flight (running away or avoiding connection).

Most of us have experienced some wounding in both our

masculine and feminine aspects. Perhaps you have noticed yourself feeling powerless in certain situations, or you may have found yourself controlling others to protect your emotional wounds. These patterns aren't who you truly are—they are expressions of pain that are asking to be healed.

But before we go any further into this subject, let us be clear about something important: what we are about to explore has nothing to do with your gender, sexuality, or physical body. Instead, we will examine two fundamental energies that exist within every human being: masculine and feminine (also known as yang and yin). These energies are not about being 'manly' or 'womanly'; each has its own unique strengths, and neither is superior to the other.

Think of them like two dancers who need to move together in harmony, but not always in equal measure. Sometimes one leads while the other follows, and their dance changes depending on what is needed in the moment. When these energies are balanced within us, we feel whole, confident, and at peace. However, when they are out of balance or wounded, they can create numerous challenges in our lives, ranging from relationship struggles to career blocks to feelings of disconnection from ourselves.

True feminine energy is not passive or weak - it is a powerful force of receptivity and creation. Healthy masculine energy is not about dominance or aggression; it is about confident action and providing structure. Understanding and healing these energies is about reconnecting with both aspects of your essential nature so you can live as your complete, authentic self.

How Imbalances Develop

From the moment we are born, we start receiving messages about how we should express our energies. Often, these messages come from well-meaning sources such as our families, schools, religious institutions, and the wider society. But they can plant the seeds of imbalance in our masculine and feminine energies. You might have been told to 'toughen up' when you were hurt, or to 'be nice' when you wanted to stand your ground. These seemingly small moments can shape how comfortable you feel expressing different aspects of your energy.

Think about the subtle (and not so subtle) messages you have received throughout your life. Maybe you learned that being strong meant never showing vulnerability, or that being caring

meant always putting others first. Our society tends to praise certain expressions of energy while dismissing or even shaming others.
Men are often encouraged to embody extreme masculine traits—being tough, competitive, and emotionally stoic. Women are frequently pushed toward exaggerated feminine traits - to be passive, nurturing to a fault, and to silence their own needs.

But it is not just about societal messages. Your personal experiences also play a significant role. Perhaps you had a parent who was overly controlling, teaching you to suppress your own power. Or maybe you experienced betrayal or hurt that led you to build walls around your heart. Trauma, big or small, can wound these qualities within you. When you are hurt while expressing one type of energy, you might unconsciously shut it down or push it to unhealthy extremes.

The challenge is that these imbalances often create a snowball effect. When one energy is wounded, you might overcompensate with the other. For example, if your feminine energy was hurt by not being heard or valued, you might swing too far into masculine energy, becoming controlling or aggressive to ensure you are never vulnerable again. Or, if your masculine energy was wounded by criticism or failure, you might retreat too far into feminine energy, becoming passive and indecisive in an attempt to avoid taking risks.

What makes this even more difficult is that these imbalances can feel normal because they are all you have known. You might not even realise you are operating with imbalanced energies until you start experiencing problems in your relationships, career, or personal life. However, understanding how these imbalances develop is the first step toward addressing and healing them. When you can see how your energies got knocked out of balance, you can start the journey of bringing them back into harmony.

Understanding Wounded Energies

When our masculine and feminine energies become wounded, they express themselves in ways that can harm both ourselves and others. These wounds often develop from past hurts, trauma, or societal conditioning that taught us to express these energies in unhealthy ways.

Wounded feminine energy often manifests as a victim mentality, characterised by feelings of powerlessness and a sense of being at the mercy of circumstances or other people. You may find yourself constantly seeking approval or validation from others, struggling to make decisions without outside input, or manipulating situations to indirectly meet your needs. This wounded energy can manifest as extreme neediness or dependency in relationships, where you lose yourself in trying to please others. You might notice yourself being oversensitive to criticism, withholding your true feelings, or using emotional manipulation to control situations.

On the other hand, wounded masculine energy typically appears as an unhealthy drive for control and dominance. When your masculine energy is wounded, you may find yourself being overly aggressive or confrontational, using criticism as a means of control, or trying to manage every aspect of your life and relationships. This can manifest as an inability to be vulnerable, a constant need to compete or prove oneself, or difficulty expressing emotions in healthy ways. You might struggle with anger management, have trouble accepting help from others, or use force (whether physical, emotional, or verbal) to get your way.

Both types of wounded energy can create significant challenges in your life. You might swing between feeling completely powerless and trying to control everything, or between being overly dependent and pushing people away. These patterns can damage your relationships, hinder your career progress, and prevent you from experiencing genuine intimacy and connection with others.
When we examine the four trauma responses mentioned in an earlier chapter through the lens of wounded feminine and masculine energies, interesting patterns emerge.

The Healthy Expression of Masculine and Feminine Energies

When your energies are unwounded and flowing naturally, they create a beautiful dance of complementary forces that enhance your life and relationships. Healthy feminine and masculine energies work together, each bringing their unique strengths to create wholeness and balance.

Healthy feminine energy expresses itself through receptivity, intuition, and creativity. When your feminine energy flows naturally, you can trust your inner wisdom and follow your intuition with confidence. You can express your emotions in balanced ways, nurture yourself and others without losing your sense of self, and remain open to life's possibilities. This energy enables you to be sensitive without being oversensitive, to love unconditionally while maintaining healthy boundaries, and to navigate life's changes with ease while staying grounded in your own truth.

Meanwhile, healthy masculine energy manifests as confident action, clear direction, and steady support. When your masculine energy is unwounded, you can set and maintain healthy boundaries, take decisive action toward your goals, and provide stability for yourself and those around you. You can be strong without being domineering, focused without being rigid, and protective without being controlling. This energy helps you move forward with courage, take responsibility for your choices, and maintain discipline as you pursue your goals.

Together, these healthy energies create a powerful foundation for living authentically. You can be both strong and tender, logical and intuitive, active and receptive. You know when to push forward and when to surrender, when to lead and when to follow. This balance enables you to respond to life's challenges with flexibility and wisdom, drawing on the exact type of energy each situation requires.

As we close this chapter, you might be reflecting on your own inner masculine and feminine energies and wondering, 'How do I bring these parts of myself into balance?' That is what we will explore in the corresponding chapter in Part 3. For now, notice which energy feels more wounded or suppressed in you. Awareness of the imbalance is the first step to restoration.

A FEELING OF EMPTINESS

Have you ever found yourself lying awake at night, scrolling through social media, looking at everyone else's seemingly perfect lives and wondering why your own life feels somehow... empty? Perhaps from the outside, everything appears to be great. Maybe you have the career, the lifestyle, all the things you are 'supposed' to have. But there's this nagging feeling that something is missing.

Or perhaps your story has been different - one of constant struggle and pushing through obstacles. You have done multiple jobs, dealt with setbacks, and fought hard for everything you have. You have learned to be strong, to survive, to make it work no matter what. Yet, despite all your resilience and determination, there is still an emptiness inside—a sense that all this surviving has left little room for actually thriving.

You are not alone. Whether you have been checking all the right boxes or fighting against the odds, many of us reach a point where we question if this is really all there is. This disconnect between your life circumstances and inner fulfilment is trying to tell you something important: you might be missing a sense of genuine purpose.

The Hollow Success

Success without meaning is like climbing a mountain only to discover there is nothing at the top - just an empty summit and the realisation you will need to climb back down. You did all that work, but for what?

This emptiness manifests in different ways for different individuals. You might notice it during your morning commute, that quiet voice wondering if this is really what you want to be doing with your life. Perhaps it hits you in those peaceful moments before sleep when you can't quite shake the feeling that you are just going through the motions. You might feel it when you achieve something significant - a promotion, a milestone, a major purchase - and the excitement fades far more quickly than you expected, leaving you feeling oddly empty.

The thing about this emptiness is that it does not make logical sense. You are either doing everything you are 'supposed to' or you have shown remarkable strength in facing life's difficulties. You might even be achieving goals that others dream about. So why doesn't it feel more satisfying? Why do you keep feeling like there must be something more?

Living Without a Compass

Living without purpose is like sailing without a destination or a compass. You might be moving, the wind might be in your sails, but are you actually going anywhere meaningful?

When you lack a clear sense of purpose:

- your days blend in a forgettable blur
- decisions become harder because there is no deeper 'why' guiding them
- you find yourself asking, 'Is this all there is?' more frequently
- motivation becomes increasingly challenging to maintain
- your energy is scattered across too many directions
- small obstacles feel disproportionately overwhelming

Without purpose, you are more vulnerable to external pressures and expectations. You might find yourself living according to others' definitions of success or constantly seeking validation from outside sources. Your worth becomes tied to achievements or possessions rather than a sense of meaning.

The Dopamine Trap

You might think happiness comes from chasing those feel-good moments - the thrill of buying something new, the rush of achieving a goal, or the excitement of starting a new relationship. And yes, these experiences give you a lovely burst of dopamine, your brain's pleasure chemical. But these surface-level highs are like riding a rollercoaster - you get that exhilarating rush to the top, but then comes the inevitable crash.

This constant seeking of dopamine hits can become a substitute for a deeper purpose. Before you know it, you are hunting for your next fix - maybe it's another shopping spree, an achievement, or a new relationship. It is an exhausting cycle that never actually fills the emptiness.

When your self-worth comes from outside yourself - how many likes your posts get, how impressed others are by your achievements, or how your success compares to others - you are stuck on what psychologists call the 'hedonic treadmill.' You set a goal, work hard to achieve it, reach it, feel good briefly, but then the feeling fades, and you need a new, bigger goal. Then, the cycle repeats.

It is exhausting. Always running, never quite arriving, and constantly needing more, bigger, better. While there is nothing wrong with enjoying life's pleasures, if you are continually chasing these temporary highs, thinking they will bring lasting fulfilment, you are missing the deeper purpose that could actually fill that emptiness.

What Keeps You Stuck in Emptiness

The Comfort Zone Prison

Your comfort zone might feel safe, but it can actually be a kind of prison that prevents you from discovering your purpose. You have decorated this prison nicely, you know where everything is, and you have got your routine sorted. However, it is still limiting your freedom to explore what might truly light you up from within. The thing about your comfort zone is that it does not always feel comfortable. Sometimes it is just familiar discomfort. We humans are creatures of habit, and we tend to prefer the discomfort we know over the uncertainty we don't. This is why many of us find ourselves in unproductive situations.

You might find yourself staying in an unfulfilling job simply because at least you know what to expect each day. Or perhaps you are keeping toxic relationships around because you are afraid of what being alone might feel like. Maybe you regularly avoid new experiences by telling yourself, 'that's just not who I am,' when, in reality, you are avoiding the discomfort of growth that might lead you to your purpose.

Disconnection from Inner Wisdom

Perhaps the biggest thing keeping you stuck in emptiness is losing touch with your own inner wisdom - that internal guidance system that knows what would truly fulfil you. In today's world, accessing this wisdom has become increasingly difficult. The constant noise of social media and technology creates a perpetual distraction, filling every quiet moment with information, opinions, and entertainment. When was the last time you sat in silence, without reaching for your phone or turning on the TV? These rare moments of stillness are often where your sense of purpose speaks most clearly.

Society's messages about who you should be also exert a

powerful influence. From a young age, we are bombarded with cultural narratives about success, happiness, and what makes a life worthwhile. These narratives shape our goals and desires in ways we might not even recognise, pulling us further from our authentic sense of purpose.

When you are disconnected from your inner wisdom, it is like trying to navigate with a broken compass. You might find yourself making decisions based on what you 'should' do rather than what feels deeply meaningful to you. Perhaps you have chosen a career path that impresses others but leaves you feeling unfulfilled, or pursued relationships that seemed promising on paper but lacked genuine connection.

Signs You Are Living Without Purpose

How do you know if you are experiencing the emptiness that comes from a lack of purpose? The signs are often subtle but unmistakable once you recognise them. You might notice you are just going through the motions each day, following predictable patterns without genuine enthusiasm or engagement—physically present but mentally elsewhere. Achievements that should feel satisfying instead leave you feeling flat, with the momentary pleasure quickly fading as you shift focus to the next goal. You may find yourself easily bored or restless, your mind constantly seeking stimulation or distraction to fill the void that purpose would otherwise occupy.

Your sense of self-worth might depend heavily on external validation—accomplishments, job titles, or bank balances—rather than an internal sense of meaning. Decision-making becomes driven by 'shoulds' rather than genuine desires, with choices based on others' expectations or appearances rather than what feels meaningful to you. When asked about what truly matters or what you are passionate about, you might struggle to find authentic answers beyond the next achievement.

Perhaps most tellingly, your life appears impressive on paper yet feels strangely empty in reality, creating a disconnect between outer success and inner experience that signals a life rich in activity but poor in purpose. This gap between how things appear and how they feel is often the most painful indicator that something essential is missing from your life.

The Real Cost of Living Without Purpose

Emotional and Physical Toll

Living without a sense of purpose takes a tremendous toll on both your mind and body. It is like walking through life carrying a heavy weight you don't need to bear. Your shoulders tense up, your jaw clenches, your stomach ties itself in knots - all because you are moving through life without the energy that comes from meaning.

This emptiness often manifests in physical symptoms: frequent headaches, persistent muscle pain, trouble sleeping despite feeling exhausted, or constant fatigue that caffeine can't seem to fix. You might experience digestive issues that come and go mysteriously or find yourself catching every cold and virus that circulates - signs of a body struggling under the burden of purposelessness.

Loss of Joy in Simple Pleasures

When you are caught up in a life without a clear purpose, you often lose the ability to enjoy life's simple moments. It is like watching a sunset through a dirty window - you can see it, but you can't really feel its warmth. You might notice subtle changes in how you experience life: food no longer tastes as vibrant as it once did, music no longer sends shivers down your spine or brings tears to your eyes, and beautiful moments seem to pass by without truly touching your heart. You find yourself constantly waiting for some future event rather than savouring the richness of now.

Spiritual Disconnection

Living without purpose creates a deep disconnect from your spiritual core - that essential part of you that knows why you are here. It is like having a beautiful garden inside you, but never taking time to tend it. This disconnection manifests as a persistent sense of emptiness, even when everything in your life appears to be going well. It is characterised by a gradual loss of touch with your deepest values and what matters to you, a missing sense of belonging to something greater than yourself, and a foggy memory of what truly lights up your heart.

The Wake-Up Call

A wake-up call can arrive when you have achieved everything you thought you wanted, only to feel hollow inside. You have got the job, the house, the relationship, and the status - but something is missing.

Or your wake-up call can come from a different place. If your life has been one long struggle - constantly pushing through obstacles and fighting to survive - then your emptiness is not about having it all. Instead, it is about bone-deep exhaustion. You yearn for peace, for ease, for just one day where you don't have to battle for every small victory.

Either way, this emptiness is actually a gift, a signal from your soul that there is more to life than going through the motions - whether those motions are climbing the success ladder or simply trying to keep your head above water.

You may notice subtle signs that you are ready for change: a growing restlessness, persistent questions that won't go away, or a yearning for something more meaningful. Or perhaps it hits you all at once - a moment of clarity where you realise, 'I can't keep living this way.

This wake-up call is life's invitation to discover your purpose. Yes, it might feel scary to move beyond the familiar emptiness into unknown territory. But there is also an exciting spark of possibility. The purposeless life has served its function - it has shown you what does not fulfil you. Now it is time to discover what it does.

In Part 3 of this book, we will explain the journey of connecting with your sense of purpose and creating a life aligned with what truly matters to you. For now, simply acknowledge that you are ready for something different - something meaningful that will fill the emptiness with genuine purpose and joy.

PART 2: THE FOUNDATION OF TIMELESS TRUTHS

As you explore the challenges holding you back from living your authentic life, you might wonder: 'Am I the first person to feel this way? Has anyone found answers to these struggles before?'

The truth is, you are walking a path that countless others have travelled throughout history. The wisdom that can help you break free from emotional baggage, find self-love, transform your relationship with money, and balance your inner energies is not new - it is ancient and timeless. For thousands of years, across diverse cultures and traditions, people have grappled with the same fundamental questions about identity, purpose, and personal transformation that you face today. They have discovered profound insights that remain remarkably relevant to modern life.

In this section, we will explore two powerful sources of wisdom that can guide your journey of rebecoming:

- First, we will dive into ancient wisdom traditions such as Buddhism, Taoism, and Stoicism, among others, that offer practical approaches to releasing what no longer serves you. These traditions provide time-tested practices for healing emotional wounds, cultivating self-love, and living with greater authenticity.
- Then, we will examine the Universal Laws that govern how energy moves in your life and the world around you. Understanding these principles gives you a framework for creating meaningful change and aligning with your true nature.

What makes these teachings so powerful is not just their age but their proven effectiveness across generations and cultures. They have helped millions before you, transforming their lives, and they can help you, too. The challenges you face aren't unique to our modern world - they are part of the human experience. And while the specific manifestations may look different today (such as social media comparison or digital overwhelm), the core issues remain the same. The good news is that the solutions are already available, having been tested and refined over centuries.

As we explore these timeless teachings, you will find they speak directly to your struggles with responsibility, emotional baggage, self-love, relationships, external control, money blocks, negative energy, inner balance, and purpose. They offer not only philosophical concepts but also practical tools that you can apply in your everyday life.

Your journey of rebecoming is both uniquely yours and part of a much larger, older story of human growth and self-discovery. Let's return to this collective wisdom to guide you forward.

ANCIENT WISDOM

While scrolling through endless new self-help techniques and quick fixes, you might wonder if your modern challenges require cutting-edge solutions. But what if the answers you are seeking have already been discovered and refined over thousands of years?

Ancient wisdom traditions have endured not through clever marketing, but because they work. They offer time-tested approaches to releasing emotional baggage, finding authentic love, breaking free from external control, and balancing your inner energies.

In the pages that follow, we will explore several powerful traditions. We recognise that there are many others from around the world that aren't included in this chapter. Our focus is on those that particularly address the themes of this book and offer practical insights for modern transformation.

It is also important to note that we are presenting specific aspects of these rich and complex traditions—those teachings that directly relate to overcoming what holds you back and reconnecting with your authentic self. Each of these wisdom paths contains centuries of knowledge that goes far beyond what we can cover here.

You won't need to master ancient languages or adopt elaborate rituals. Think of these traditions as a toolkit filled with practical instruments for transformation that you can select from and integrate into your everyday life in ways that feel right for you.

Core Wisdom Themes Across Traditions

As we explore different ancient wisdom traditions, you will notice certain universal themes emerge. These common threads have emerged across cultures and centuries because they resonate with fundamental human experiences. Let us examine these core themes before exploring how each tradition addresses them uniquely.

Breaking Free from Conditioning

All ancient wisdom traditions recognise that much of your suffering comes from living according to external programming rather than your authentic nature. This conditioning—from family, education, media, and culture—creates internal conflict

when it does not align with your true self.
Whether it is called 'delusion' in Buddhism, 'conditioning' in Zen, or 'programming' in modern terms, these traditions offer paths to recognise and release these external influences, allowing you to live more authentically.

Embracing Your Wholeness

Ancient traditions consistently teach that healing comes from embracing your entire self—including the parts you have been taught to reject or hide. Rather than trying to eliminate 'negative' aspects, these traditions show how to integrate all elements of your experience into a cohesive whole. This might be expressed through balancing yin and yang in Taoism, integrating shadow aspects in Jungian psychology (which draws from many ancient traditions), or seeing all experiences as sacred in Tantra.

Finding Inner Authority

Each wisdom tradition, in its own way, guides you back to your inner authority, rather than seeking validation and direction from the outside world. They teach that true wisdom comes from within, even as they offer practices and frameworks to support this journey. Whether through meditation in Buddhism, self-inquiry in yoga, or applying philosophical principles in Stoicism, these paths help you distinguish between authentic inner guidance and external pressures.

Transforming Rather Than Suppressing

Ancient wisdom recognises that suppressing difficult emotions and experiences does not lead to healing. Instead, these traditions offer ways to transform challenging energies into something beneficial. From transforming the Four Poisons into the Four Immeasurables in Buddhism to transmuting energy in Hermeticism, these approaches demonstrate how to work with rather than against the challenging aspects of life.

Redefining Responsibility

These traditions reframe responsibility from a burden of obligation to an empowering choice. They teach that while you can't control external circumstances, you always maintain choice in how you respond. This shift—whether expressed through Stoic philosophy, Buddhist mindfulness, or Hermetic principles—places the locus of control within you rather than in outside forces.

Balancing Opposing Forces

All ancient traditions recognise the importance of balance between complementary energies—often described as masculine and feminine, but extending beyond gender to encompass qualities like action and receptivity, strength and surrender, or logic and intuition. These traditions teach that true power comes from integrating these seemingly opposite qualities rather than emphasising one at the expense of the other.

Cultivating Self-Love Through Self-Knowledge

Ancient wisdom paths consistently teach that true self-love stems from self-knowledge and acceptance, rather than trying to improve oneself to meet external standards. They offer various practices for developing this awareness and compassion toward yourself.

Let's examine how each tradition uniquely approaches these common themes.

Buddhism

Have you ever felt like you are just going through the motions in life, following rules and expectations that don't actually feel right for you? Buddhism offers insights about this exact struggle and provides practical tools to break free.

Unique Buddhist Approaches

The *Four Noble Truths* provide a systematic framework for understanding and releasing suffering:

1. Acknowledging suffering: Recognising when you are living inauthentically.
2. Understanding the cause: Seeing how attachments and cravings create suffering.
3. Recognising liberation is possible: Knowing you can break free.
4. Following the practical path: Using the Eightfold Path as your guide.

The *Eightfold Path* offers specific practices for each aspect of life:

- Right Understanding: Recognising conditioning.
- Right Intention: Committing to authenticity.
- Right Speech: Communicating truthfully.
- Right Action: Making choices aligned with your true self.
- Right Livelihood: Creating work that reflects your values.
- Right Effort: Applying appropriate energy to breaking free.
- Right Mindfulness: Developing awareness of when you are acting from conditioning.
- Right Concentration: Focusing on what truly matters.

Transforming Difficult Emotions through practices that develop the *Four Immeasurables*:

- loving-kindness (metta)
- compassion (karuna)
- appreciative joy (mudita)
- equanimity (upekkha)

Buddhism uniquely emphasises a middle path—avoiding both indulgence and harsh self-denial—making it especially relevant for those who tend toward either extreme in their approach to growth.

Zen

Zen offers a direct, experiential approach to freedom that focuses on breaking through conceptual thinking to direct experience. While rooted in Buddhism, Zen's distinctive methods target the thinking mind itself.

Unique Zen Approaches

Zazen (seated meditation) helps you observe your mind's patterns without getting caught in them, creating space between yourself and your programming.

Direct experience over concepts: Zen emphasises 'tasting' life directly rather than living through mental concepts about life, using:

- koan practice (paradoxical questions that can't be solved through logical thinking)
- mindful physical activities like archery, calligraphy, or tea ceremony

- direct teacher-student transmission beyond words

Radical acceptance: Rather than seeing self-love as self-improvement, Zen suggests true self-love is fully accepting yourself exactly as you are now.

Simplicity: Zen directly counters materialistic programming through practices of simplicity and sufficiency, asking 'How much is enough?'

Zen's unique emphasis on non-dualistic thinking helps you move beyond either/or programming to embrace paradox and complexity.

Taoism

Like water finding its natural path, Taoism teaches aligning with your true nature rather than forcing yourself into external moulds.

Unique Taoist Approaches

Wu Wei (non-forcing action): Moving with your authentic inclinations rather than pushing against your nature, finding the path of least resistance.

Balance of Yin and Yang: Embracing both receptive (yin) and active (yang) qualities regardless of gender, recognising that these complementary forces exist within everyone.

Nature as teacher: Using natural systems as models for authentic living, observing how rivers flow, plants grow, and seasons change without struggle.

The Middle Way: Finding sufficiency between excess and lack, especially regarding possessions and desires.

Taoism uniquely emphasises working with, rather than against, your nature—not forcing change, but allowing natural transformation through alignment with the Tao (the natural way).

Native American

While representing hundreds of distinct traditions, many Native American wisdom paths share insights about interconnection and wholeness.

Unique Native American Approaches

The Medicine Wheel: Using this sacred circle to understand how physical, mental, emotional, and spiritual aspects must be in balance for true wellness.

Mitákuye Oyás'iŋ (All Are Related): Recognising interconnectedness with all life, challenging the programming of separation and competition.
Ceremony and Ritual: Using intentional practices to mark transitions, express gratitude, and connect with deeper meaning.

Right Relationship: Maintaining harmony, balance, and reciprocity in all connections rather than seeking control.

Honour for Both Joy and Suffering: Seeing all experiences as teachers with purpose in your journey.

These wisdom traditions uniquely emphasise a relationship with the natural world as essential to authentic living—a perspective particularly relevant in our environmentally disconnected modern context.

Tantra

Tantra offers a radical approach that sees your entire self—including aspects you have been taught to reject—as expressions of something sacred.

Unique Tantric Approaches

Transformation Rather Than Rejection: Working with 'negative' energies rather than fighting against them, seeing everything as potential fuel for awakening.

Sacred View of Body and Pleasure: Honouring physical experiences as pathways to awareness, challenging shame-based programming.

Energy Work Through Chakras: Working with energy centres to release stored programming and expand consciousness.

Integration of Masculine and Feminine: Balancing and honouring both Shiva (masculine) and Shakti (feminine) energies within everyone.

Tantra uniquely emphasises that the path to liberation goes

through experience rather than around it—directly countering programming that certain aspects of life are 'too worldly' or must be transcended.

Stoicism

This Greek and Roman philosophy offers practical wisdom for taking responsibility for your life regardless of external circumstances.

Unique Stoic Approaches

Dichotomy of Control: Focusing entirely on what you can control (your choices, responses, and values) while accepting what you cannot control (external events and others' actions).

Character Development Over External Success: Finding satisfaction through developing virtue rather than accumulating possessions or status.

Practical Exercises: Using specific practices like negative visualisation (imagining losing what you value) to build resilience and appreciation.

Voluntary Discomfort: Deliberately practising mild discomfort to break programming that ties your worth to comfort and convenience.

Stoicism uniquely emphasises rational examination of beliefs and emotions, making it especially helpful for those whose programming manifests as reactive emotional patterns or irrational beliefs.

Hermeticism

This ancient tradition teaches the connection between your inner world and outer reality through principles like 'as above, so below' and 'as within, so without.'

Unique Hermetic Approaches

Mental Transmutation: Changing your thoughts and beliefs to transform your experience, recognising the causal relationship between inner and outer worlds.

Seven Hermetic Principles: Using Universal Laws like Correspondence, Vibration, and Polarity to understand how reality operates.

Working with Subtle Energies: Practices for sensing and directing subtle forces beyond the physical.

The Middle Way Between Science and Spirituality: Integrating rational understanding with mystical experience.

Hermeticism uniquely emphasises the creative power of your consciousness, teaching that your inner state directly affects what you manifest in your life—a principle now echoed in quantum physics and neuroplasticity research.

Yoga

While often thought of in Western culture as simply about physical postures, yoga is actually a comprehensive system for integrating body, breath, and mind.

Unique Yogic Approaches

The *Yamas and Niyamas*

Ethical principles that directly support authentic living:

- Ahimsa (non-violence): Treating yourself and others with compassion.
- Satya (truthfulness): Speaking your truth.
- Asteya (non-stealing): Not denying your authentic needs.
- Brahmacharya (energy management): Using your life force wisely.
- Aparigraha (non-attachment): Letting go of programmed attachments.
- Saucha (purity): Clearing mental and emotional clutter.
- Santosha (contentment): Finding peace with what is.
- Tapas (self-discipline): Building new patterns aligned with your true self.
- Svadhyaya (self-study): Distinguishing between programming and authentic nature.
- Ishvara Pranidhana (surrender): Releasing the need for control.

Integration of Body, Breath, and Mind: Using physical practices (asana), breathwork (pranayama), and meditation to create wholeness.

Balancing Solar and Lunar Energies: Specific practices to balance warming/activating qualities with cooling/receptive qualities within each person.

Yoga uniquely emphasises the body as a vehicle for transformation, recognising that programming is stored not just in the mind but in the physical body and energetic system.

Ayurveda

As yoga's sister science of holistic health, Ayurveda recognises that authentic living requires understanding your unique constitution.

Unique Ayurvedic Approaches

Individual Constitution (Dosha): Identifying your unique combination of Vata (air/space), Pitta (fire/water), and Kapha (earth/water) energies to understand your natural tendencies.

Personalised Practices: Tailoring diet, lifestyle, and healing approaches to your specific constitution rather than following generic advice.

Seasonal and Cyclical Awareness: Adjusting practices according to time of day, season, and life stage to stay in balance.

Treating Imbalance Rather Than Symptoms: Addressing the root causes of physical and emotional issues through constitutional understanding.

Ayurveda uniquely emphasises that your path to authenticity must honour your specific nature. What works for others might not work for you, and what works for you might change throughout your life.

These ancient traditions remind us that the challenges we face today—feeling disconnected from our true selves, struggling with external pressures, seeking meaning and purpose—are not new. Humans have been wrestling with these questions for millennia, and in their wisdom, we can find timeless guidance for our very modern lives.

THE UNIVERSAL LAWS

Have you ever felt like there is a hidden set of rules that make the world work? Well, you are right, they are called Universal Laws. They are always working, whether we believe in them or not. They are like invisible strings that tie everything together. Just as a musician tunes their instrument to create beautiful music, we can also tune ourselves to these Universal Laws to cultivate a life full of growth, meaning, and spiritual happiness.

As you embark on your journey of rebecoming, it is helpful to understand the Universal Laws that govern our existence. These laws aren't like the laws of physics you learned in school. Instead, they are more like guidelines that explain how the universe works on a deeper level.

Many of these laws have been recognised and taught in ancient wisdom traditions for thousands of years, though often using different terminology. As we explore these universal principles, we will highlight how they connect with the timeless teachings from various cultures and traditions.

The Law of Mentalism

Everything Begins in the Mind

Have you ever noticed how your thoughts shape what happens in your life? That is the Law of Mentalism at work. This simple yet powerful law reveals that everything begins in our minds before showing up in our experiences.

Your mind is like a garden. Whatever seeds you plant there - whether thoughts of confidence or doubt, abundance or scarcity - will eventually grow into your reality. The thing is that you didn't plant many of these thought-seeds—your parents, teachers, friends planted them, and even TV shows and social media.

These planted thoughts can become the emotional baggage and limiting beliefs we talked about earlier. The belief that 'I'm not good enough' or 'Money is hard to come by' first exists as a thought before it becomes your lived experience.
What makes this law empowering is that once you realise that your thoughts create your reality, you gain the power to change them. Instead of blaming your boss, your partner, or the economy for your problems, you can look at the mental patterns that might be creating your experience.

This is especially true with money. Do you catch yourself thinking thoughts like 'rich people are greedy,' 'I'll never have enough,' or 'I don't deserve abundance'? These mental patterns actually shape your financial reality. By changing these thoughts, you can transform your experience with money.

Ancient Wisdom Connection: This principle is reflected in Buddhism's emphasis on how our thoughts create our reality and Hermeticism's fundamental principle of 'The All is Mind.' Buddhism teaches that our suffering comes from our perceptions and thought patterns, while Zen practices help us observe how our mind creates our experienced reality.

The Law of Oneness

We Are All Connected

Have you ever felt a deep connection with someone you just met? Or maybe you have experienced moments in nature where you suddenly felt part of something much bigger than yourself? These are glimpses of what the Law of Oneness is all about.

This law tells us that underneath all our apparent differences, we are all connected. It is as if we are waves on the ocean - each of us appears separate on the surface, but deep down, we are all part of the same water.

This simple truth challenges one of the biggest lies we have been programmed to believe - the lie of separation. When you feel isolated, unworthy, or like you are in constant competition with others, you are experiencing this illusion rather than the deeper reality of connection.

Think about how this affects your understanding of love. Many of us carry a false idea that love is about possessing another person, controlling them, or using them to fill our emptiness. These are all programmed misunderstandings. Real love flows naturally when you recognise your connection with others and with all of life.

Ancient Wisdom Connection: This principle is beautifully expressed in the Native American concept of 'Mitákuye Oyás'iŋ' (meaning 'All Are Related') and Buddhism's teachings on interdependence. Native traditions emphasise our fundamental interconnection with all life, while Buddhism teaches that nothing exists independently - everything arises in relation to everything else.

The Law of Vibration
Everything Is Energy

Imagine you are at a concert. Even with your eyes closed, you can feel the music moving through your body. That is because sound travels in waves that literally vibrate the air and everything they touch - including you. The Law of Vibration works on this simple principle: everything in the universe is energy vibrating at different frequencies.

This includes your thoughts, emotions, and beliefs. When you are feeling joyful, loving, or peaceful, you are vibrating at a higher frequency. When you are feeling afraid, ashamed, or resentful, you are vibrating at a lower frequency. It is similar to the difference between a flute's high, light notes and a bass guitar's low, heavy ones.

This explains why negative emotions and programmed patterns feel so heavy - they literally vibrate at a lower, denser frequency. Have you ever noticed how emotions like resentment, guilt, and fear seem to weigh you down? Or how being around certain people leaves you feeling drained and heavy? That is their vibrational frequency affecting yours.

The good news is that as you heal and release your old programming, your vibrational frequency naturally increases. You begin to feel lighter, clearer, and more energised. And the exciting part is that you then start to attract experiences that match this lighter state. It is like tuning a radio to a different station - suddenly you are picking up a whole different broadcast.

Ancient Wisdom Connection: This principle is expressed in yogic traditions through the concept of different states of consciousness having distinct vibrational qualities. Tantra works directly with energy, teaching that everything from our emotions to our chakras operates at different frequencies that can be transformed through conscious awareness.

The Law of Polarity
Everything Has Its Opposite

Have you ever noticed how life seems full of opposites? Hot and cold, light and dark, joy and sadness. The Law of Polarity reveals something fascinating about these opposites - they are not truly separate entities at all. They are actually two ends of the same stick.

Think about temperature. Hot and cold seem like complete opposites, but they are really just different points on the same temperature scale. There is no exact moment when 'cold' suddenly becomes 'hot'- it is all one continuous spectrum. This simple truth challenges how we have been programmed to see the world in black-and-white, either/or terms. Life is not so rigid. Most things exist somewhere along a spectrum rather than at extreme ends.

Take, for example, masculine and feminine energies. We are often taught that these are completely opposite and separate - that men should be one way and women another. However, the Law of Polarity reveals that these energies are complementary expressions along a continuum. Each of us contains both energies regardless of our gender.

Ancient Wisdom Connection: This principle is central to Taoism's concept of yin and yang - complementary forces that exist within everything. Taoism teaches that these apparently opposite forces are actually interconnected and interdependent. Similarly, Tantra recognises the integration of seemingly opposite energies as essential to wholeness.

The Law of Rhythm

Everything Flows in Cycles

Have you noticed how everything in nature moves in cycles? The seasons change from spring to winter and back again. The tides flow in and out. The moon waxes and wanes. Even our bodies follow rhythms - we breathe in and out, our hearts beat in a rhythm, and we move through cycles of wakefulness and sleep.

The Law of Rhythm teaches us that these natural cycles also apply to our emotional healing journey. Breaking free from old programming is not a straight line from start to finish. It is more like a spiral where you move through periods of incredible insight and growth, followed by times of integration, and sometimes what feels like going backwards - though at this point, you are actually just processing at a deeper level.

Understanding this rhythm helps you navigate the ups and downs of healing without feeling overwhelmed. The days when you feel like you have taken two steps back are just part of the natural rhythm, not a sign of failure.

Ancient Wisdom Connection: Native American traditions use the medicine wheel to represent life's cyclical nature, while

Taoism emphasises flowing with natural cycles rather than resisting them. Both traditions teach that understanding and honouring these natural rhythms leads to greater harmony and less struggle.

The Law of Relativity

Nothing Is Good or Bad on Its Own

Have you ever noticed how something can seem amazing or terrible depending on what you compare it to? A cool spring day feels wonderful after a harsh winter, but chilly after a hot summer. A modest pay rise might feel disappointing if your coworker got twice as much, but fantastic if you were expecting nothing at all. That is the Law of Relativity at work.

This simple law tells us that nothing is good or bad on its own - everything depends on how you perceive it and what you compare it to. This directly challenges all those programmed judgments that create so much suffering in your life.

Think about how your sense of who you are was formed. You probably spent years comparing yourself to siblings, friends, celebrities, and societal standards. 'Am I pretty enough? Smart enough? Successful enough?' All these comparisons created a false identity based on where you thought you stood relative to others, rather than on who you truly are.

Ancient Wisdom Connection: Buddhism teaches that suffering comes from our judgments rather than reality itself. The concept that nothing is inherently good or bad is also reflected in Stoicism's approach, which focuses on how we perceive events rather than on the events themselves.

The Law of Cause and Effect

What You Put Out Comes Back

Have you planted seeds in your garden? If you plant tomato seeds and care for them properly, you will get tomatoes—not cucumbers or roses. That is the Law of Cause and Effect in action. Simply put, what you put out comes back to you.

Some traditions refer to this as Karma, but it is not a mysterious force that punishes or rewards you. It is a natural principle that shows every action generates a corresponding reaction. This universal law directly addresses responsibility: your current circumstances result from past causes, including your thoughts, beliefs, and actions.

This law explains why the programmed patterns we have discussed tend to persist. Each time you react from your conditioning - maybe by people-pleasing or losing your temper - you strengthen that pattern and create effects that reinforce it. It is like walking the same path through a field over and over until it becomes a well-worn trail that is easy to follow automatically.

But the empowering part is that this same principle means new choices create new effects. By taking responsibility for your choices now, you set in motion different outcomes.

Ancient Wisdom Connection: This principle is central to Buddhism's concept of karma and Hermetic teachings on cause and effect. It is also reflected in Stoicism's emphasis on taking responsibility for what we can control (our choices) while accepting what we cannot.

The Law of Correspondence

As Within, So Without

Have you ever noticed how your home or workspace often reflects your inner state? When you feel chaotic inside, your space tends to become messy too. When you feel balanced and clear, your environment often reflects that balance. This is the Law of Correspondence in action - your outer world reflects your inner world.

This simple yet powerful law teaches that your external reality—your relationships, work, health, and finances—mirrors your inner landscape of beliefs, emotions, and identity. That is why internal healing naturally creates external transformation, often in ways that seem almost magical.

This law illustrates why attempting to control others or circumstances is ultimately ineffective. It is like trying to fix a crooked shadow by manipulating the shadow itself, when what you really need to do is straighten the object casting the shadow. True change must begin within.

Ancient Wisdom Connection: This principle is directly expressed in Hermeticism's axiom, 'As above, so below; as within, so without.' This is also reflected in yoga's understanding that internal states manifest in external experiences, and in Zen's emphasis on inner work that creates outer change.

The Law of Attraction

Like Attracts Like

Have you ever noticed how some people seem to repeatedly experience the same problems? Or how certain individuals always seem to 'get lucky' in life? The Law of Attraction helps explain these patterns.

This law suggests that you naturally attract experiences that align with your dominant thoughts, feelings, and beliefs - especially those that lie beneath the surface of your awareness. It's as if your inner world is a magnet, drawing in circumstances that resonate with what's already within you.

This explains why the programmed patterns we have discussed tend to persist. If you were programmed to believe 'relationships are hard' or 'money is always tight,' you will unconsciously attract situations that prove these beliefs true. It is not because the universe is punishing you; it is because your unconscious programming acts like a homing beacon, attracting experiences that match it.

What is interesting about this law is that focusing on what you don't want often brings more of it. By shifting your focus from what you fear to what you desire, you change what you attract.

Ancient Wisdom Connection: While not explicitly named 'attraction' in ancient teachings, this principle appears in Buddhist concepts of how our mental patterns create our reality and in Hermetic teachings about resonance. The principle that 'energy flows where attention goes' appears in many wisdom traditions.

The Law of Assumption

What You Assume Becomes Your Reality

Have you ever had the experience of assuming someone was upset with you, only to find yourself acting strangely around them, which then made them even more upset? Or perhaps you thought a situation would be difficult, and that assumption made you so nervous that you created the very difficulty you feared?

This is the Law of Assumption at work. It tells us that what you assume to be true becomes your experience. Your assumptions about yourself, others, and life create a lens through which you see everything—and this coloured perception shapes what you experience as reality.

Think of it like wearing tinted glasses. If you put on red-tinted glasses, everything looks red. Wear blue, and suddenly the world appears blue. Your assumptions work the same way - they colour everything you see and experience.

The problem with this is that you did not consciously choose many of your strongest assumptions. They were installed through your family, education, media, and culture.

Ancient Wisdom Connection: This principle relates to Buddhism's teachings on how our perceptions shape our reality and Stoicism's emphasis on how our judgments about situations affect us more than the situations themselves.

The Law of Gender

Balancing Masculine and Feminine Energies

Have you ever noticed how some men seem afraid to show sensitivity, while some women feel they need to hide their strength? Or how certain people seem to be all action with no reflection, while others are all ideas with no follow-through? These imbalances point to what the Law of Gender is all about.

This law reveals that true wholeness comes from balancing both masculine and feminine energies within yourself - regardless of your biological sex or gender identity. It directly challenges the programming that separates these complementary energies and assigns them based on whether you were born male or female.

Let's be clear about what these energies actually are. Masculine energy represents the active, directive, and assertive aspects of consciousness - the part of you that takes action, sets boundaries, and makes decisions. Feminine energy embodies the receptive, creative, and nurturing qualities - the part of you that listens to intuition, goes with the flow, and connects deeply with others.

Both of these energies are essential for wholeness. An imbalance in either direction creates limitation and suffering.

Ancient Wisdom Connection: This principle is central to Taoism's concept of yin and yang, Tantra's integration of Shiva (masculine) and Shakti (feminine) energies, and Hindu concepts of balanced energetic principles. All these traditions teach that wholeness comes from integrating rather than separating these complementary forces.

The Law of Perpetual Transmutation

Energy Is Always Changing Form

Have you ever watched ice melt into water and then evaporate into steam? Or seen a caterpillar transform into a butterfly? These are perfect examples of the Law of Perpetual Transmutation in action - the principle that energy is constantly changing form.

This simple but powerful law tells us that nothing stays the same forever - including your programmed patterns, negative emotions, and limiting beliefs. Everything is always in a state of becoming something else. This universal principle offers real hope because it shows us that transformation is not just possible - it is actually the natural order of things.

Consider what this means for emotional healing. Those feelings of trauma, grief, or anger that seem so overwhelming? They are not permanent states but energy that can be transmuted into wisdom, compassion, and strength. Rather than trying to suppress your painful emotions, you can transform their energy into something more helpful.

Ancient Wisdom Connection: This principle appears in Tantra's approach to transforming energy rather than suppressing it. It is also reflected in Buddhist practices that transform difficult emotions into compassion and wisdom, and alchemical traditions of transmutation.

The Law of Action

Knowledge Must Be Applied

Have you ever read a great self-help book, felt inspired for a few days, only to see nothing actually change in your life? That is because information without application rarely leads to transformation. The Law of Action addresses this common pitfall.

This law teaches us that real change requires more than just awareness or intention - it demands concrete steps in the physical world. While all the inner work we have discussed is essential, without action, it remains just potential energy rather than a manifest reality.

Think of it like cooking a meal. You can read recipes all day long and have all the right ingredients in your kitchen, but until you actually start chopping vegetables and turning on the stove, no one is going to get fed. The Law of Action reminds us that doing is just as important as knowing and being.

Ancient Wisdom Connection: This principle is reflected in yoga's emphasis on both practice (action) and knowledge, Buddhism's Eightfold Path, which includes right action alongside right understanding, and Stoicism's focus on the practical application of philosophical principles.

The Law of Compensation

You Receive in Proportion to What You Give

Have you ever noticed how putting genuine effort into something often yields rewards that exceed your expectations? This is the Law of Compensation - a simple but powerful truth about how life works when you live authentically.

Think of it like planting a garden. When you take the time to prepare the soil, plant the seeds, water regularly, and pull the weeds, you don't just get the vegetables you planted - you also get healthier soil, visiting butterflies, and the joy of working with your hands. Compensation goes well beyond the obvious harvest.

The same thing happens when you do the inner work we are talking about. As you release emotional baggage, cultivate self-love, and break free from old patterns, you create space for good things to flow into your life. These rewards may include increased energy, better relationships, improved health, greater peace, or even financial abundance.

This is not about magical thinking - it is about cause and effect. When you show up as your true self in your life and relationships, people respond differently to you. When you honour your true needs instead of pushing through exhaustion, your body has a chance to heal. When you value yourself appropriately, others tend to value you more, too.

Ancient Wisdom Connection: This principle relates to Buddhist concepts of reaping what you sow and the Hermetic principle of cause and effect. It is also reflected in Taoist teachings about natural balance and reciprocity.

--

As we have explored these Universal Laws, you may have noticed that they don't operate in isolation. They work together to create a harmonious system that governs our experiences.

For example, the Law of Mentalism (thoughts create reality) works in conjunction with the Law of Attraction (like attracts like) and the Law of Correspondence (as within, so without) to demonstrate how your inner world influences your outer experience. The Law of Polarity (everything has its opposite) and the Law of Rhythm (everything flows in cycles) work together to explain the natural fluctuations of life.

The Universal Laws and Ancient Wisdom traditions both point to the same fundamental truth: we live in an intelligent, interconnected universe that operates according to consistent principles. By aligning yourself with these principles, you open to the natural flow of life and reclaim your ability to create from your authentic self rather than from old programming.

PART 3: RETURN TO WHO YOU TRULY ARE

'The path to the light seems dark.' - Lao Tzu

To this point, you have seen what has been holding you back in life, understood Ancient Wisdom traditions, and learned the Universal Laws. Now we come to the most transformative part of our journey together - returning to who you truly are. Not the person your career demands you to be, not the face you show at the school run, and definitely not the carefully curated version you may present on social media. We are talking about your real, soul-level self.

What has truly been holding you back is not living in accordance with the Ancient Wisdom and Universal Laws that have guided human flourishing for millennia. When you live disconnected from these timeless principles, you experience the inevitable consequences: relationships that drain rather than nourish you, work that depletes rather than fulfils you, and a nagging sense that something essential is missing.

Perhaps you have been operating against the Law of Rhythm, pushing yourself to constant productivity without honouring the natural cycles of effort and rest. Or maybe you have violated the Law of Polarity by trying to eliminate all challenges rather than understanding their necessary role in your growth. You might have overlooked the Law of Correspondence, focusing on changing external circumstances while ignoring the inner patterns creating them. These disconnections from universal principles create the very struggles you have been experiencing.

The answer is not found in another self-improvement strategy or productivity hack. The answer is to return to who you really are – a being naturally aligned with these Universal Laws. Your authentic self intuitively understands the interconnectedness the Native Americans recognised, the balance of opposites that Taoism celebrates, and the transformative power of awareness that Buddhism teaches. The path forward is not about learning something new but remembering something ancient, something your soul has always known.

This return involves reconnecting with timeless wisdom, but applying it thoughtfully to modern living. You do not need to retreat to a monastery or live in a forest to embody these principles. You can honour the Law of Gender by balancing masculine drive with feminine receptivity in a corporate leadership position. You can apply Stoic principles of focusing on what you can control while navigating social media's constant comparisons. You can practice Buddhist non-attachment while building a successful business in today's economy.

Think back to when you were a child, before the world told you who to be or how to act. Remember that natural confidence? That ability to love freely, to express yourself without hesitation, to find wonder in the smallest things? That wasn't just a phase of childhood - it was you, in your purest form, naturally aligned with universal principles. That essence is still within you, waiting to be rediscovered.

The truth that might be challenging to hear is that the path back to yourself is not always smooth or comfortable. Just like building physical strength requires resistance and challenge, emotional and spiritual growth demands that we face our struggles head-on. You cannot bypass the difficult parts any more than you can get fit without ever breaking a sweat.

Consider this question: How can you truly understand freedom if you have never felt trapped? How can you fully appreciate joy if you have never navigated sadness? The very experiences that have felt like obstacles on your path—the challenging career transitions, the relationship struggles, the moments of self-doubt—are not just random hardships. They are actually essential parts of your journey back to yourself.

Maybe you have experienced that gut-wrenching feeling when a long-term relationship ended, or that sleepless anxiety when your career took an unexpected turn. Perhaps you have achieved everything society told you would bring fulfilment - the successful business, the beautiful home, the perfect family - only to find yourself still feeling somehow empty and incomplete. These are not failures or wrong turns on your path. They are actually valuable teachers, showing you what truly matters to your soul.

The chapters ahead will guide you through this transformation. We will explore how to heal old wounds that have kept you disconnected from your authentic nature. You will learn how to balance and heal both your masculine and feminine energies, tap into your natural life force, and align with your soul's purpose. We will work with ancient wisdom that has helped people find their way home to themselves for thousands of years.

This is not about becoming someone new - it is about remembering who you have always been beneath the layers of protection, adaptation, and social conditioning. It is about reclaiming the gifts, the joy, and the power that are your birthright. Every step you take toward your authentic self is a step toward greater freedom, deeper love, and a more meaningful life.

Think of it like climbing a mountain. Yes, there will be challenging terrain. Yes, there will be moments when you question whether it is worth it. But each difficult step makes you stronger, and the perspective from the summit will transform how you see everything - including yourself.

The journey back to yourself takes courage. It means being willing to look honestly at patterns that might have served you well in your career or relationships but no longer align with your deeper truth. It means being willing to feel uncertain, to let go of control, to trust in something bigger than your carefully laid plans.

But here is the beautiful truth: you would not be reading these words if you were not ready. The very fact that you are here, engaging with this material, shows that your soul is already calling you home. Trust that inner knowing. Trust that the struggle and uncertainty you might be feeling are not signs that something is wrong - they are actually indicators that you are on the right path.

Remember - the goal isn't to become some kind of enlightened being who never experiences doubt or difficulty. As long as you are human, you will experience the full spectrum of human emotions and challenges. The difference is in how these experiences affect you. With each step of this journey, you will become more capable of staying connected to who you really are, even in challenging times.

Are you ready to return to your true self? To rediscover that essential spark that has been within you all along? To let your struggles transform into stepping stones toward the real you?

The path ahead might seem dark at times, but that is exactly where the light begins to shine through. Let's take this journey together.

OWN IT ALL

Ancient Wisdom & Universal Laws:

- *The Stoics and Buddhists understood what the Law of Cause and Effect reveals: while you cannot control life's first arrows, you always maintain sovereignty over your response. As Marcus Aurelius wrote, 'You have power over your mind—not outside events,' for when you claim ownership of your reactions, you transform from a victim of circumstance to an author of experience.*

- *Zen wisdom teaches that presence—fully inhabiting each moment with a beginner's mind—frees you from the prison of fixed narratives about your past. This ancient wisdom illuminates the path of rebecoming: own it all with clear-eyed presence, release the stories that bind you, and you free yourself to create without limits.*

You learned earlier in this book that there is something incredible about the universe and your place in it. Everything that exists, literally everything, is thought-based. It is all energy, vibrating at different frequencies. And your thoughts are part of this cosmic dance, too. They are creating your reality moment by moment, day by day.

Think about that for a second. Your life, exactly as it is right now, is a reflection of your thoughts and the energy you have been putting out into the universe. The good stuff, the not-so-good stuff, and everything in between - you have created it all with your mind.

Now, you might be thinking. 'Wait a minute, are you saying I'm responsible for everything in my life?' And the answer is yes. This may feel overwhelming. It is often easier to blame circumstances, other people, or simply bad luck when things are not going our way. But the liberating truth is that taking full responsibility for your life is the most empowering thing you can do.

Why? Because if you have created your current reality with your thoughts and energy, that means you have the power to create a new one. You are not just along for the ride - you are in the driver's seat of your life.

This chapter is all about owning it. All of it. The wins and the losses, the ups and the downs. It is about looking at every aspect of your life and saying, 'I created this with my thoughts and energy, and I can create something different if I choose to.' Now, this does not mean beating yourself up over things you wish were different. That is not what taking responsibility is about. Instead, it is about acknowledging your role in creating your current reality so that you can call on your power to create the future you desire.

Remember, taking responsibility is not about blame; it is about empowerment. It is about recognising that you have the power to shape your reality with your thoughts and energy, starting right now. Are you ready to take control of your life and create the life you truly desire?

You have heard it before: 'Take responsibility for your life.' But what does that really mean? At its core, taking responsibility means accepting that your life is yours. While others' actions and circumstances can affect you, ultimately, your life is your responsibility. This might seem harsh, but it is actually empowering. One major obstacle to taking responsibility is the tendency to blame others. Blaming is common in our society, but it leaves you powerless. When you blame, you are saying, 'My life is in someone else's hands.' But when you take responsibility, even in tough situations, you are declaring, 'I have the power to shape my life, regardless of circumstances.'

It is crucial to understand the difference between the healthy expression of emotions and unhelpful blame. Venting can be healthy to a point, helping you process difficult situations. But be careful not to let venting turn into blaming. If you are holding grudges or constantly revisiting the same complaints, you have crossed into unhelpful blame territory.

Taking responsibility means understanding that it is not anyone else's job to improve your life. Your partner is not responsible for your happiness, your boss is not obligated to ensure you are fulfilled at work, and society does not owe you success. These realisations might be uncomfortable, but they are liberating. If no one else is responsible for making your life better, you have the power to do it yourself.

This shift in perspective may be uncomfortable at first, but it is precisely in this discomfort that real growth occurs. You may need to confront difficult truths, make challenging changes, acquire new skills, or reassess your relationships. It won't always be easy, but this discomfort signifies growth and increased self-reliance.

Taking responsibility also means facing reality honestly. It is about seeing things as they are, not as you wish they were. This honesty with yourself and others is powerful. It allows you to identify areas for improvement, celebrate genuine successes, and build trust in relationships. As you embrace honesty and face reality, it is important to redefine success. True success is the growth you achieve. Every time you learn something new, overcome a challenge, or push past your comfort zone, you are succeeding.

Living in the present is crucial for taking responsibility. It is not about dwelling on past mistakes or worrying about future problems. It is about focusing on what you can do right now. The past is gone, the future has not arrived, but the present is where you have the power to act and make changes.

Finally, taking responsibility means accepting the consequences of your choices. Every action you take (or don't take) has results. Owning these consequences, good or bad, is part of being responsible. It is about saying, 'I made this choice, and these are the results. What can I learn from this?'

Remember, taking responsibility is not about blame or guilt. It is about recognising your power to shape your life. It is understanding that while you cannot control everything that happens to you, you can control how you respond. It is about moving from 'Why is this happening to me?' to 'What can I do about this?'

As you continue to practice taking responsibility, you will likely notice profound changes in your life. You may feel more empowered and in control of your destiny. Your relationships might improve as you stop expecting others to make you happy. You might find yourself making progress towards goals that once seemed out of reach.

Your journey starts now, in this present moment. Embrace it, own it, and watch your life transform.

'Responsibility is not a burden. It is the power to create the life you want.'

BREAK FREE FROM BEING CONTROLLED

Ancient Wisdom & Universal Laws:

- *'Make the best use of what is in your power, and take the rest as it happens,' taught Epictetus, revealing what the Law of Mentalism confirms: true freedom begins within your own mind.*

- *The Taoist concept of wu-wei reminds us that liberation comes not through struggle but by aligning with your authentic nature.*

- *Zen wisdom teaches that when you observe thoughts without attachment, external manipulation loses its grip. This ancient understanding illuminates the path of rebecoming: as you reclaim sovereignty over your mental and energetic boundaries, you break free from the invisible chains that once directed your life.*

Imagine waking up one day and realising that many of your choices—from the career you pursued to the way you spend your free time—were not really your choices at all. Instead, they were shaped by external forces, including societal expectations, family pressures, manipulative relationships, and addictive technology.

This is the reality for many of us. We live in a world where external control is so subtle and pervasive that we often mistake others' voices for our own. We chase goals planted in our minds, follow paths laid out by culture rather than by calling, and spend our precious energy trying to meet expectations we never consciously accepted.

This chapter is your roadmap to breaking free—a journey from unconscious compliance to conscious choice. Using the Recognise, Resist, Reclaim, and Rebuild framework, we will explore practical strategies to help you identify controlling influences, build healthy resistance, reclaim your autonomy, and rebuild your life based on your genuine values and desires.

Are you ready to break the invisible chains and start living on your own terms? Let's begin.

Recognise: Seeing The Unseen Controls

Developing Self-Awareness

Freedom begins with awareness. You cannot break free from control you do not recognise.

Start paying attention to your decisions—both big and small—and the emotions behind them. When you make a choice, pause and ask yourself: 'Is this truly my desire, or am I responding to external pressure?' Notice when you feel anxious, resentful, or obligated about a decision. These emotions often signal that external forces, not your authentic self, are driving your behaviour.

> *Reflection Exercise: Decision Origins*
>
> For the next week, keep a small notebook handy. Each time you make a significant decision (what to wear, how to respond to a request, how to spend your evening), jot down:
>
> - the decision you made
> - how you felt about it (before and after)
> - who or what might have influenced this choice
> - whether this choice aligns with your values and desires
>
> After a week, review your notes. Look for patterns. Do certain people or situations frequently influence your choices? Do you regularly make decisions that do not align with your authentic desires? These patterns reveal the external controls in your life.

Recognising Different Forms of Control

External control takes many forms, some obvious and others incredibly subtle.

- *Social and Cultural Expectations.* Society bombards us with messages about how we should live: the milestone ages for marriage, homeownership, or career advancement; the 'right' way to parent; how our bodies should look; what success means. These expectations seep into our consciousness until we mistake them for our own desires.
- *Family Conditioning.* Family patterns and expectations are among the most powerful influences on behaviour. Perhaps you pursued a career to please your parents, adopted their political views without question, or

continued unhealthy relationship patterns you witnessed growing up.
- *Digital Manipulation.* Modern technology is designed to capture and control your attention. Social media algorithms, addictive app features, and constant notifications manipulate your behaviour very effectively.
- *Manipulative Relationships.* Control can be exercised by partners, friends, or colleagues who use guilt, obligation, fear, or emotional manipulation to influence your choices and behaviour.
- *Media and Marketing.* Advertising does not just inform you about products—it creates artificial needs and shapes your self-image to sell solutions to problems you did not know you had.

Self-Assessment: Rate each area from 1-10 based on how much external control you experience:

- Family expectations (____/10)
- Social/cultural pressure (____/10)
- Digital/technology influence (____/10)
- Relationship dynamics (____/10)
- Media/marketing impact (____/10)
- Workplace expectations (____/10)

The areas with the highest scores deserve your immediate attention.

Understanding Internal Resistance

Even when we recognise external control, we often resist breaking free. This resistance is not weakness—it is a natural response to change and uncertainty.

Common forms of internal resistance include:

- fear of rejection or disapproval
- comfort with the familiar, even if it is limiting
- identity attachment (who am I if not the person others expect me to be?)
- uncertainty about alternatives
- legitimate concerns about consequences

Reflection Questions:

- What would be the worst consequence of defying an external expectation?

- What parts of your identity feel threatened by the idea of change?
- What beliefs do you hold about your capacity to make good decisions?

Recognising both external control and your internal resistance to change establishes the foundation for breaking free. Now, let us explore how to actively resist these controlling influences.

Resist: Developing Your Freedom Muscles

Cultivating Critical Thinking

Once you have recognised external control, critical thinking becomes your first line of defence. This means questioning the messages you receive instead of passively accepting them.

When you encounter an expectation, opinion, or 'should' statement, practice asking:

- Who benefits from me believing this?
- What evidence supports this idea?
- Does this fit with my experiences and values?
- What assumptions underlie this message?
- Would I reach this conclusion independently?

For example, if you feel pressured to own a home by a certain age, examine this expectation. Is homeownership necessary for your happiness, or is it a societal norm or family expectation? If an advertisement makes you feel inadequate without a product, question whether it is addressing a genuine need or creating an artificial one.

This questioning habit helps you distinguish between external pressures and your authentic desires.

> *Practice Exercise: Message Dissection.*
>
> Choose a magazine ad, social media post, or piece of advice you recently received. Write down any implied assumptions and expectations it contains. Then write a counter-argument challenging each assumption. This exercise helps strengthen your critical thinking skills.

Setting and Maintaining Boundaries

Boundaries are the practical expression of your autonomy—

they define where others' influence ends and your sovereignty begins.

Start by clarifying your values and non-negotiables. What matters most to you? What are you unwilling to compromise on? Once clear on these boundaries, communicate them clearly to others.

Effective Boundary-Setting Techniques:

1. Use 'I' statements: Instead of 'You are always controlling,' try 'I need to make this decision independently'.
2. Start small: Practice setting boundaries in less threatening situations before tackling major relationships.
3. Be consistent: Inconsistently enforced boundaries invite continued testing.
4. Expect resistance: When you change patterns, others will often push back. Prepare for this reaction rather than being surprised by it.
5. Non-negotiable time: Create sacred space in your schedule that belongs only to you.

Boundary Script Templates:

- 'I value our relationship, but I need to make this decision based on what works for me.'
- 'I understand you have strong feelings about this, but I am going to handle it my way.'
- 'I am not available for [activity/conversation]. I can offer [alternatives] instead.'
- 'I need some time to think about this before I respond.'

Remember, setting boundaries is not about controlling others—it is about taking responsibility for your own well-being and choices.

Breaking Free from the Digital Trance

Technology offers incredible benefits, but many digital platforms and devices are specifically designed to capture and control your attention—often at the expense of your autonomy and well-being.

Digital Freedom Plan:

1. Conduct a digital audit: Track your technology use for 1

week. Note which apps you use, how much time you spend, and how you feel before, during, and after each session.
2. Identify your digital vulnerabilities: Which platforms cause you to lose track of time? Which ones leave you feeling worse afterwards? These are your priority areas for establishing control.
3. Create structural barriers: Delete the most problematic apps, use blocking software during certain hours, or keep devices out of your bedroom.
4. Practice intentional use: Before picking up your device, state your purpose aloud: 'I am checking my email for important messages, then putting my phone down.'
5. Establish tech-free zones and times: Designate spaces (like your bedroom) and times (like the first hour after waking) as technology-free.
6. Find alternative dopamine sources: Technology companies have engineered their products to trigger dopamine (the brain's feel-good chemical) releases that keep you engaged. Counter this by seeking healthier sources of pleasure and satisfaction, such as engaging in physical activity, immersing yourself in nature, pursuing creative endeavours, or engaging in meaningful conversations.

Mini-Challenge: Try a 24-Hour Digital Detox. Notice how many times you habitually reach for your devices and what emotions arise when you cannot access them. This awareness alone can weaken technology's grip on your attention.

Navigating Social and Peer Pressure

The desire to belong is fundamental to human psychology, making social pressure one of the most powerful forces shaping our behaviour. Resisting this pressure requires awareness and the courage to act.

Ways to Maintain Autonomy in Social Settings:

- Prepare your responses: Before entering situations where you expect pressure, decide in advance how you will respond.
- Use the broken record technique: Repeat your position calmly without feeling obligated to explain or justify yourself.
- Find your people: Cultivate relationships with those

who respect your autonomy and support your authentic choices.

- Practice mental rehearsal: Visualise yourself maintaining your boundaries in challenging situations.
- Delay tactics: When pressured, say 'Let me think about it' to create space for your authentic decision.

Script Ideas:

- 'That does not work for me.'
- 'I have decided to handle this differently.'
- 'I appreciate your concern, but I have made my choice.'
- 'I know this is different from what you expected, but it is important to me.'

Remember, true connection comes from authentic self-expression, not compliance with others' expectations.

Reclaim: Taking Back Your Power

Reclaiming Your Decision-Making Authority

After recognising control and developing resistance, the next step is actively reclaiming your decision-making power.

Start with small choices where the stakes feel manageable. Each autonomous decision strengthens your 'choice muscle' and builds confidence in your judgment.

The *CHOICE* Method for Authentic Decisions:

- **C**larify what matters to you in this situation
- **H**onour your feelings and intuition
- **O**ptions—identify at least three possibilities
- **I**nvestigate whether they fit with your values
- **C**onsider legitimate impacts on others
- **E**xecute your decision with confidence

Decision Journal Prompt: Think of a decision you are currently facing. Apply the CHOICE method, writing your thoughts at each step. Notice how this process differs from your usual decision-making.

Healing from Controlling Relationships

Some controlling influences go beyond normal social pressure into manipulation or abuse. Recognising and healing from these relationships requires special attention and often professional support.

Warning Signs of Controlling Relationships:

- You frequently doubt your perceptions or memory.
- You feel you must 'walk on eggshells' to avoid problems.
- Your needs and boundaries are regularly dismissed.
- You are isolated from supportive friends or family.
- You feel responsible for the other person's emotions.
- Your independence is undermined or discouraged.

If you recognise these patterns, prioritise your safety and wellbeing:

- Contact trusted friends, family, therapists, or support groups.
- If physical safety is a concern, identify safe places, set aside emergency resources, and know who to call.
- Keep a private record of incidents that disturbed you.
- Be clear about what is and is not acceptable, and hold to these boundaries.
- A qualified therapist can help you navigate complex relationship dynamics and healing.

Remember, you deserve relationships that respect your autonomy and contribute to your well-being. Breaking free from controlling relationships may be challenging, but the freedom on the other side is worth it.

Practising Mindful Autonomy

Mindfulness—the practice of being present in the moment without judgment—is a powerful tool for reclaiming autonomy. By developing awareness of your thoughts, feelings, and bodily sensations, you create space between the stimulus and the response, where true choice resides.

Mindful Autonomy Practices:

- Mindful decision pauses: Before making choices, take three conscious breaths. Notice any sensations, emotions, or thoughts that arise. Ask: 'What is truly mine at this moment?'
- Body awareness check-ins: Throughout the day, especially when feeling pressured, scan your body. Tension, constriction, or discomfort often signals that you are acting against your true desires.
- Thought labelling: When thoughts arise about what

you 'should' do, mentally label them as 'external expectation' or 'authentic desire' to create separation and choice.

- Values alignment meditation: Regularly reflect on your core values and how your current choices align with them.

5-Minute Mindful Autonomy Practice:

- Sit comfortably and focus on your breath for 1 minute
- Bring to mind a decision or situation where you feel external pressure
- Notice where you feel this in your body
- Ask: 'What do I truly want in this situation?'
- Notice any answers that arise without judgment

Regular mindfulness practice helps you distinguish between external noise and your authentic voice, creating the foundation for genuine autonomy.

Rebuild: Creating Your Self-Directed Life

Discovering Your Genuine Values

Once you have begun breaking free from external control, a crucial question often arises: 'If I am not living according to others' expectations, then what do I truly want?'

This is where rebuilding begins—by discovering and clarifying your authentic values.

Values Discovery Process:

- Reflect on moments when you felt most alive, fulfilled, and authentic. What values were you expressing?
- Notice what triggers your strongest negative reactions, such as anger. These often point to violated values.
- Consider the people you most admire. What qualities do they embody?
- Imagine you are at the end of your life, looking back. What would make you feel your life was well-lived?
- From these explorations, identify 3-5 core values that feel most essential to your authentic self.

For each core value you identify, list:

- How might this value express itself in your daily life?

- One small action you can take this week to live in accordance with this value.
- How living this value might differ from your current patterns.

When your choices align with your values, external influences lose their impact.

As you apply the strategies in this chapter, remember that breaking free from external control is not a destination but a continuous journey of awareness, choice, and shifting.

External control mechanisms are constantly evolving, becoming more sophisticated and subtle. New social pressures emerge, technology develops novel ways to capture attention, and relationships change. Maintaining your autonomy requires ongoing vigilance and adaptation.

Yet with practice, this vigilance becomes second nature. You will develop an increasingly sensitive awareness of when something feels authentically aligned versus when it is externally imposed. You will build confidence in your ability to make choices based on your values rather than others' expectations. And you will discover the deep satisfaction that comes from living a self-directed life.

The journey is not always easy. You will face resistance—both from others who benefited from your compliance and from your own habitual patterns. You will sometimes slip back into old ways of being. But with each conscious choice, each boundary set, each authentic expression, you strengthen your freedom muscles.

And as you do, you will discover something remarkable: the more you live from your authentic core, the less effort it takes to resist external control. Like water flowing in its natural channel, your life begins to move with an effortless power when aligned with your true nature.

LET GO OF YOUR EMOTIONAL BAGGAGE

Ancient Wisdom & Universal Laws:

- *The Buddha's Four Noble Truths offer profound insight into emotional baggage: life contains suffering (dukkha), this suffering has a cause (our attachments and the stories we cling to), suffering can be transcended, and there is a path to freedom. What ancient traditions call the journey from burden to freedom.*

- *The Law of Perpetual Transmutation reveals that your emotional wounds are not static but dynamic forces awaiting transformation.*

- *The Zen understanding of impermanence reminds us that nothing is fixed, including your relationship to past pain; what feels permanent today can shift and transform tomorrow. It also teaches us to 'be with' our suffering, moving toward pain rather than away from it initiates the alchemy that converts suffering into wisdom. Rather than trying to eliminate all discomfort, you learn to face your emotional baggage directly, reducing the 'optional suffering' that comes from the stories you tell yourself about unfairness or permanence.*

- *The Law of Oneness shows that healing your wounds contributes to collective healing, as we share one fundamental essence despite appearances of separation. When you develop loving kindness toward your own pain and struggles, you naturally extend greater empathy and compassion to others navigating their own healing journey.*

- *Through the Law of Relativity, you discover that your experience of any painful memory exists only in relation to your perspective, giving you the power to reframe your past with a beginner's mind—approaching your history with curiosity rather than rigid conclusions, open to new possibilities for understanding and growth. By releasing attachment to fixed views about what your trauma 'means' about you, you create space for transformation. Your deepest wounds, through the Law of Polarity, contain their opposites—the very gifts and strengths you seek on your path of rebecoming.*

As we know from the earlier chapter, your emotional baggage

did not accumulate overnight. Each piece was packed with care - a protection here, a defence mechanism there. Perhaps you've packed away your trust after a betrayal, stored your vulnerability after being hurt, or silenced your authentic voice after being criticised one too many times.

At first, this baggage might have served you well. That caution helped you avoid further hurt. That perfectionism drove you to achieve. That people-pleasing tendency helped you navigate complex professional relationships. But now? Now, these same strategies that once protected you are keeping you from the very things you want most: deeper connections, greater authenticity, and more meaningful success.

Deep within, you might feel a growing awareness that something needs to change. Perhaps it shows up as:

- a persistent feeling that, despite your achievements, something is missing
- exhaustion from maintaining the perfect image
- a quiet longing for more authentic connections
- an increasing sense that you are ready for a different way of being

This awareness is not random - it is your inner wisdom speaking. Like a compass pointing true north, it is trying to guide you toward wholeness. The very fact that you are reading these words suggests you are ready to listen to that inner voice.

Any transformation requires honest assessment, so consider:

- What patterns keep repeating in your life despite your best efforts to change them?
- Where do you find yourself compromising your truth to maintain peace or success?
- What parts of yourself have you hidden away in an effort to fit in or achieve?
- What old stories about yourself no longer serve the person you are becoming?

This is not just a reflection - it is reconnaissance. You are taking stock of what you have been carrying, maybe for the first time in years. Some of these bags might be so familiar that you have forgotten they are optional. Others might be so painful that you have avoided looking at them altogether.

Releasing your emotional baggage requires courage. It means examining those carefully packed bags, deciding what to keep and what to let go. It means developing new ways of moving through the world - ones that do not require such a heavy load.

This process is not always easy. Your protection system might resist as you embark on this. It might bring up fears such as:

- 'What if I need these defences later?'
- 'Who will I be without these familiar patterns?'
- 'What if looking at old hurts brings back the pain I have been trying to avoid?'

These fears are normal. They are just your protection system doing its job. However, what is important to remember is that you are not the same person who first packed these bags. You are stronger now, wiser, with more resources and resilience than you had before.

The journey ahead is about lightening your load, not abandoning all protection. It is about consciously choosing what to carry forward and what to leave behind. With each piece you release, you will find more energy for the things that truly matter, such as your dreams and your relationships.

Change begins with a decision. Not a perfect plan, not a guarantee of success, but a wholehearted commitment to your own growth. This commitment might look like:

- deciding that your peace of mind is worth more than your familiar patterns
- choosing self-awareness over automatic reactions
- valuing being genuine more than appearance
- trusting that you can handle whatever emerges as you unpack these old bags

Think of healing as becoming whole again, which is actually what the word 'heal' means at its root. But becoming whole does not mean rushing to fix everything at once. This is a careful process of examining what you carry, keeping what serves you, and gently releasing what no longer serves you. Some experiences and tools from your past are valuable—they have helped shape your wisdom and resilience. The goal is not to erase your history or travel through life without any baggage. Instead, it is about consciously choosing what to carry forward into your future and what to leave behind.

So, are you ready to begin? To examine what you have been carrying and choose, perhaps for the first time, what you want to keep? The path ahead holds challenges, yes, but it also promises something precious: the freedom to move through life with just what you need, no more and no less.

Healing Your Emotional Wounds Yourself

We have been conditioned to believe that healing emotional wounds requires a professional - a therapist, counsellor, or mental health expert. While these professionals can provide valuable support, the truth is that you have the innate capacity to heal yourself. This understanding of our natural healing abilities dates back to ancient times, as reflected in traditions across cultures and continents. In any case, there simply are not enough mental health professionals to support everyone seeking help, and many people face barriers to accessing professional support, whether due to cost, time constraints, or availability.

Importantly, you are the foremost expert on your own life. You were there when these wounds were created. You understand the nuances of your experiences in a way no one else can. You also have a deep well of wisdom within you - an inner knowing that has been there all along, even if it has been buried under layers of protection and pain.

This is not about being broken and needing to be fixed. And your emotional wounds are not signs of weakness - they are evidence of your humanity. They often developed as intelligent responses to challenging situations. Just as your body knows how to heal a physical wound, your psyche has an innate capacity for emotional healing. The key is to create the right conditions and understand the process.

Being vulnerable with yourself is central to this healing journey. It requires courage to look honestly at your wounds and gentle determination to work through them. But remember - you created these protective layers for good reasons at the time, and you have the power to release them when they no longer serve you mindfully.

In the pages that follow, we will explore a specific process and techniques for this self-directed healing. You will learn practical tools for accessing your inner wisdom and working through emotional wounds at your own pace. These are not mystical abilities or rare talents - they are natural human capacities that you already possess. Like any skill, they simply need to be understood and practised.

What is particularly powerful about learning to heal yourself is that these innate emotional healing skills are with you for life. Unlike depending solely on external support, you can use these abilities anytime, anywhere. You become your own source of healing and support.

Let us explore these innate healing skills and how they work together.

Your Awareness Skills

These are the skills that help you notice and understand what is happening within and around you. Think of them as your inner compass.

- *Inner Awareness* is like having an internal monitoring system. It helps you tune into what is happening in your body - those gut feelings, that tightness in your chest, or the warmth in your heart.
- *Outer Awareness* helps you understand how your environment affects you. It is your ability to notice when certain situations, places, or people trigger emotional responses. This skill enables you to create spaces and circumstances that support your healing.
- *Mindfulness* is your 'be here now' skill. It helps you stay present with your experiences without getting lost in them. Think of it as being able to observe your thoughts and feelings like clouds passing in the sky - you see them, but you don't have to chase after them.
- *Clarity* is like having a bright flashlight in a dark room. It helps you see what is really going on inside, separating your true self from the emotional baggage you have been carrying.

Your Nurturing Skills

These skills enable you to cultivate a safe and supportive inner environment for healing.

- *Kindness* is your self-compassion ability. It is about treating yourself with the same gentleness you would offer a dear friend who is hurting. When you notice pain or sadness, try saying to yourself, 'It's okay to feel this way. I'm here for you.'
- *Self-soothing* is your ability to find peace within, even when the world around you is chaotic. Think of it as having a calm lake inside you that you can visit whenever you need to centre yourself.
- *Patience* reminds you that healing is not a race. It is your

'take it slow' wisdom that allows you to move at your own pace without pushing or rushing.

- *Belonging* connects you to something bigger than yourself - whether that is other people, nature, or a higher power. It reminds you that you are not alone on this journey.

Your Courage Skills

These skills enable you to face challenges and persevere when things get tough.

- *Bravery* gives you the strength to face the scary parts of yourself - the memories, feelings, or thoughts you have been avoiding. Remember, being brave does not mean you are not afraid; it means you are willing to move forward despite the fear.
- *Self-belief* is your 'I've got this' power. It is the part of you that knows you are capable of healing, even when things get tough. This confidence helps you trust your ability to grow and change.
- *Resilience* is like having a steady flame inside you that keeps burning even when things get challenging. It helps you keep going, one small step at a time.

Your Transformation Skills

These skills enable you to discover new paths forward and derive meaning from your experiences.

- *Curiosity* is your ability to stay open-minded instead of judgmental. When you become curious about your thoughts and feelings, asking 'I wonder why I reacted that way?' can help you uncover the roots of your emotional baggage without getting stuck in self-criticism.
- *Creativity* helps you think outside the box and find fresh approaches to old problems. Perhaps you express your feelings through art or create unique rituals to release old hurts. This skill makes your healing journey more engaging and effective.
- *Vision* is your 'big picture' ability. It helps you see beyond your current feelings to the larger story of your life. This wider view can help you understand your emotional baggage in a new, more helpful way.
- *Light-heartedness* brings a sense of joy and play to your healing journey. It helps you remember that even serious inner work does not always have to feel heavy.

> Sometimes, approaching your healing with a lighter touch can lead to profound insights.

Remember, all these skills work together, supporting and enhancing each other. You might find that some feel stronger than others right now, and that is perfectly normal. The key is to recognise that you already have these abilities within you. With practice and patience, you can strengthen all of them, creating a robust toolkit for your healing journey.

Taking Care of Yourself While You Heal

'When wild animals get hurt, they don't try to tough it out. They find a cosy, safe spot to rest and let their bodies heal. They stay there as long as they need to, without feeling bad about it or trying to push themselves too hard.'

Healing your emotional wounds takes courage and care. Just like you would not expect a physical wound to heal if you kept poking at it, emotional healing needs gentle attention and the right conditions to unfold.

When you are working with deep emotions, it is easy to be overly self-critical. You might criticise yourself for having certain feelings or try to rush the process. But self-criticism only adds to your emotional baggage. What you really need during this process is self-compassion - treating yourself with the same kindness you would offer a good friend, in other words, be your own best friend.

Being kind to yourself creates a safe space for emotions to surface and heal. It helps you view your struggles as part of being human, rather than as personal failings. Most importantly, it provides you with the emotional security to confront difficult feelings without becoming overwhelmed.

> Try this simple practice when you are feeling overwhelmed: Pause what you are doing. Place a hand over your heart. Take three deep breaths. Say to yourself, 'This is hard right now, and that's okay. I'm here for myself.' This small gesture of self-kindness can help you feel supported as you move through the healing process.

Remember, healing is not a race. Like those wise animals who rest when they are hurt, give yourself permission to take breaks, move at your own pace, and create the conditions you need to heal fully.

Head-to-Heart Healing

What we are about to describe next is not a modern form of psychotherapy. This is an ancient approach to emotional healing that people have practised for centuries across cultures and continents. Head-to-Heart Healing draws from timeless wisdom traditions and Universal Laws that govern human consciousness and transformation.

Long before the advent of modern psychology, people understood how to release emotional wounds and return to wholeness through this natural process. From indigenous healers to Eastern mystics to Western contemplatives, this fundamental pathway to emotional freedom has been walked by countless individuals throughout history.

While this practice may sound simple, it is deeply powerful. The evidence for its effectiveness is not just anecdotal. Each element of the process is supported by contemporary academic research, which we have detailed in the appendix for those interested in the science behind it.

As authors, we have personally experienced profound healing through this practice, moving from emotional struggle to genuine peace and freedom. We have also witnessed its transformative effects on the lives of others we have shared this work with.

The process is called Head-to-Heart Healing because the term captures the journey your emotional wounds must take to heal. Emotional wounds originate from thoughts and experiences that create painful emotional imprints. The healing process begins in the mind through self-awareness and understanding as you recognise and make sense of your wounds. However, true healing requires moving beyond intellectual understanding to emotional integration—feeling the buried emotions, releasing old thoughts, and allowing space for new, healthier emotional patterns to emerge. This journey from understanding to feeling, from recognition to release, creates lasting transformation. While your mind illuminates the path to healing, it is your heart that completes the journey.

What makes Head-to-Heart Healing unique is that it bridges ancient wisdom with practical application for modern life. It is not about complex techniques or spiritual bypassing. Instead, it offers a clear pathway for releasing emotional baggage and returning to your natural state of wholeness.

Step 1: Recognise Your Emotional Wounds

So, how do you begin this journey of healing your emotional baggage? Like any meaningful journey, it begins with a single step—and that step may be simpler than you think. You don't need to dive into the deep end or relive painful memories right away. Instead, you begin by simply looking at what's there with gentle curiosity.

Before you can heal something, you need to know it is there. This first step involves becoming aware of your emotional wounds and acknowledging how they manifest in your life. Remember the two guardians we discussed earlier - your Wolf and Bear? Well, now it is time to understand what they have been protecting gently. Deep in the forest of your inner world, they have been standing guard over your wounded Deer - those tender, vulnerable parts of you that got hurt and have received their fierce protection.

Like turning on a light in a dark room - suddenly you can see the patterns and beliefs they created to keep you safe. You will start to notice what triggers your protection system, understand your automatic reactions, and identify the stories you have been telling yourself to stay in control.

This is not about judging or fixing anything yet - it is simply about seeing what is there and appreciating that all these patterns served a purpose at one time.

Finding Your Hidden Wounds

Like an archaeologist carefully uncovering ancient artefacts, discovering your emotional wounds requires patience, dedication, and the right tools. These wounds often lie buried beneath layers of protective behaviours and coping mechanisms, making them challenging to identify. But understanding where you are hurt is the first crucial step toward healing.

Think of your emotional wounds as stories written in invisible ink - they are constantly influencing your life, but you need special techniques to make them visible. Sometimes these wounds show up as recurring patterns in your relationships, sudden emotional reactions that seem out of proportion, or protective behaviours that may have served you in the past but now hold you back.

There are several powerful methods you can use to bring these hidden wounds into the light. Each approach offers a different way to understand your emotional landscape, like holding up various mirrors to see yourself more clearly. Some methods involve working with others who can help reflect what they see, while others are practices you can do on your own through careful self-observation and reflection.

In this chapter, we will explore different methods for uncovering your emotional wounds:

- The Guardians Method - learning to read the clues your protection responses leave behind.
- Who's Doing the Talking? - a way to identify which guardian is active and protecting you at any particular moment.
- The Introspection Method - gently exploring your inner world through self-reflection.
- The Mindfulness Method - developing awareness of your patterns through present-moment observation.
- The Trigger Tracking Method - documenting and analysing your emotional reactions.
- The Mirror Method - using your relationships as reflections of your inner world.
- The Heyoka Method - working with a trusted person who can help illuminate your blind spots.
- The Speak Freely Method - working with a trusted person who listens deeply to you to uncover hidden patterns.

Each of these methods offers a unique pathway to deeper self-understanding. You might find that some resonate more strongly with you than others, or that different methods work better at different times in your healing journey. Try them and see which works best for you. The key is to approach this exploration with curiosity and compassion, remembering that these wounds developed for good reasons, even if they no longer serve you.

The Guardians Method

Your Wolf and Bear leave clues about the emotional wounds they are protecting. Think of these guardians as treasure maps - their behaviours, reactions, and strategies can lead you right to the buried pain they have been protecting all this time.

Recognising Wolf Patterns

When your Wolf is on high alert, it reveals important information about your past hurts. Each careful rule and boundary it creates typically guards a specific emotional wound:

- If your Wolf has a strict 'never depend on anyone' rule, there might be old wounds around abandonment or betrayal.
- When it insists 'always be perfect,' it could be protecting you from wounds of criticism or not meeting others' expectations.
- If it maintains 'keep everyone at arm's length,' there might be trust wounds from times you were hurt after letting someone in.
- When it demands 'never show weakness,' look for wounds around vulnerability being used against you.
- If it enforces 'always be prepared for the worst,' there may be wounds from times you were caught off guard and hurt.

Watch for how your Wolf patrols your life. Does it obsessively plan everything to prevent surprises? That might point to times when unexpected events left you feeling helpless or unsafe. When it tries to control how others see you, it could be protecting you from old shame or judgment wounds. If it keeps you busy and productive all the time, it might be guarding against wounds of feeling worthless or undeserving of rest.

Bear Reactions as Emergency Flares

Your Bear reacts to triggers like emergency flares - they light up exactly where the pain is. Each of its four responses points to different kinds of wounds:

When your Bear fights - lashing out or taking risks - look for wounds around:

- feeling powerless or unheard
- having your boundaries violated
- being controlled or manipulated
- having your voice silenced
- feeling trapped or cornered

If your Bear runs (through drama, addictions, or constant busyness), it might be running from:

- overwhelming grief or loss

- deep-seated shame
- fear of rejection or abandonment
- painful memories or trauma
- feelings of inadequacy or failure

A freezing Bear - disconnecting or going numb - often guards overwhelming trauma wounds. Look for:

- times when you felt completely helpless
- situations where you could not escape
- experiences that were too much to process
- moments when you felt utterly alone
- periods when you had to shut down to survive

When your Bear appeases - people-pleasing and losing itself in others' needs - it usually protects wounds around:

- not feeling worthy of love just as you are
- having to earn affection through performance
- fear of conflict or disapproval
- never feeling good enough
- having your needs dismissed or ignored

<u>Who's Doing the Talking?</u>

A powerful way to identify which guardian is active is by becoming aware of what you are saying and thinking. This 'Who's Doing the Talking?' approach helps you connect this to a specific guardian and the underlying wound.

When your Wolf is speaking:

- you hear planning, strategising, and 'what if' thinking
- your thoughts focus on potential future dangers or problems
- you are creating rules, boundaries, or escape plans
- you are calculating risks and trying to maximise safety
- you hear thoughts like 'I need to prepare for...' or 'I should avoid...'

If your Wolf is creating elaborate plans to prevent discomfort, ask what emotional wound it might be protecting. Perhaps there were times when you were caught unprepared and hurt, or when unexpected events left you feeling overwhelmed.

When your Bear is speaking:

- you hear reactive, emotional language

- your thoughts involve blame, criticism, or judgment of others
- you provide defensive justifications for your behaviour
- you are focused on immediate threats or perceived attacks
- you hear thoughts like 'they always...' or 'i never should have...'

If your Bear is criticising someone or blaming others, look deeper for the emotional wound beneath. Is there an old hurt around feeling disrespected or unheard? Does this reaction protect you from feeling vulnerable or wrong?

Wolf voices often protect wounds around:

- unexpected losses or betrayals
- times when you were unprepared and hurt
- experiences of chaos or instability
- situations where you lacked control
- moments when security was suddenly threatened

Bear voices often protect wounds around:

- feeling disrespected or dismissed
- having your boundaries violated
- being criticised or judged harshly
- feeling powerless or controlled
- having your voice silenced

As you notice these patterns in your internal dialogue or external conversations, take a moment to get curious about them. When you catch yourself speaking or thinking in a certain guardian's voice, pause and ask:

- Which guardian is doing the talking right now?
- What might this guardian be trying to protect me from?
- What emotional wound could be underneath this protective voice?
- What need wasn't met in my past that created this wound?
- What would my Owl (your wise, integrated self) say about this situation?

Consider what past experiences might have taught your guardians to react this way - there is usually a story behind each protective response. Think about what might feel threatening about handling things differently - your guardians often resist change because they are worried about old hurts repeating themselves.

Remember, your guardians developed these responses for good reasons. Each protective behaviour or thought pattern, no matter how frustrating it might feel now, came from a place of trying to keep you safe. By understanding their language and behaviours, you can compassionately uncover and begin healing the wounds they have been safeguarding. This awareness is the first step toward expressing gratitude to your guardians for their service while learning new ways to feel safe in the world.

As important as it is to recognise when Wolf and Bear are speaking, becoming familiar with your other inner voices can enrich your self-understanding and healing journey.

When your Deer is speaking:

> *Your emotional self expresses itself honestly and sensitively. It speaks the language of genuine feeling. You will hear it in statements that acknowledge emotions directly: 'I feel sad right now,' or 'This makes me happy.' The Deer's voice can be tender, vulnerable, and present—expressing both pleasant and uncomfortable feelings without judgment or analysis. When your Deer is speaking freely rather than being protected or suppressed, you are likely connecting with your natural capacity for emotional honesty. Listen for the Deer in your moments of authentic connection, when you express what truly matters to your heart.*

When your Raven is speaking:

> *The analytical Raven brings the gift of perspective and intellectual clarity. You will recognise its voice when your thoughts take flight above immediate emotional reactions, seeking patterns and meaning. 'I notice this situation links to several others in my past,' or 'From a broader perspective, I can see how this works.' The Raven helps you make sense of experiences through conceptual understanding. While this ability is valuable, notice when the Raven might be circling high above to avoid the direct emotional experience below. If your Raven is constantly intellectualising painful situations or turning emotions into abstract concepts, it might be protecting you from times when your feelings were overwhelming or dismissed as irrational.*

When your Owl is speaking:

> *The Owl represents your integrated, wise self—where intellect and emotion, caution and courage find balance. You will hear the Owl's voice when you respond to life with grounded wisdom that acknowledges both feelings and facts. 'I notice I'm feeling anxious, and I recognise this pattern from before,' or 'This situation is challenging, and I can approach it with both care and clarity.' The Owl does not avoid difficulty nor react impulsively to it. Instead, it sees clearly in the darkness, offering perspective without disconnection. When the Owl speaks, you are accessing your natural wisdom—the part of you that can hold space for all your other voices while guiding you toward genuine wellbeing.*

Each of these voices has value in your inner ecosystem. The goal is not to silence any of them, but to recognise who is speaking when, understand what lies behind what they say, and gradually allow your Owl's integrative wisdom to guide the conversation. With practice, you will develop an inner community where all voices are heard and honoured, but where healing—rather than protection—becomes the primary focus.

<u>The Introspection Method</u>

One of the most effective ways to recognise your emotional wounds is through gentle self-exploration. Think of this like being a kind detective investigating your own inner world. Instead of just reacting when you feel triggered or notice yourself using familiar coping strategies, you can pause and look more deeply at what is happening.

> When you notice yourself having a strong emotional reaction or falling into protective patterns—perhaps pushing people away, trying to control everything, or shutting down—take a moment to pause. Find a quiet space where you will not be interrupted. Take a few deep breaths to centre yourself. Then, with genuine curiosity, ask yourself these questions:
>
> - What am I trying to protect myself from right now?
> - When have I felt this way before?
> - What experiences in my past might have taught me to react this way?
> - What need wasn't met back then that I am still trying to fulfil?

For example, if you notice yourself keeping everyone at a distance, you may discover an old wound related to trust or abandonment. Or if you frequently freeze in social situations, you might uncover past experiences where you felt exposed or humiliated.

Remember, this is not about judging yourself - these protective responses were developed for good reasons. Instead, think of this as gathering information with compassion. You are simply trying to understand what lies beneath these patterns so you can begin the journey of healing.

Keep a small notebook handy, or use a note-taking mobile app, to jot down what you discover. Over time, you will start to see patterns emerge, helping you identify the core wounds that have shaped your protective behaviours.

<u>The Mindfulness Method</u>

You cannot change what you cannot see. This method helps you shine a light on the patterns, beliefs, and emotions that have been running on autopilot in your life, often without your awareness.

Creating Your Space
Find a quiet time in your day - perhaps early morning or just before bed - when you can spend 15-20 minutes in uninterrupted self-observation. You do not need any special equipment or setting, just a commitment to look honestly at yourself.

The Practice
Set a timer for 15 minutes. Sit comfortably and start by taking a few deep breaths to centre yourself.

Watch Your Mind
Instead of trying to control or change your thoughts, become a curious observer. Notice:

- What thoughts keep popping up?
- What worries or concerns repeat themselves?
- What stories do you tell yourself about your life?
- What judgments arise about yourself or others?

Track Your Body
Your body often knows things before your mind does. Pay attention to:

- where you hold tension

- what sensations arise when you think about certain people or situations
- any physical reactions to specific thoughts
- areas that feel blocked or uncomfortable

Notice Your Emotions
Emotions are like weather patterns moving through you. Observe:

- What emotions come up most frequently?
- Which emotions do you tend to push away?
- How you react to different emotional states
- What triggers specific emotional responses?

Write It Down
After each session, give yourself 5 minutes to write down:

- patterns you noticed
- recurring thoughts or worries
- physical sensations that stood out
- emotions that surfaced
- any insights or connections you made

Look for the Threads
Over time, start looking for the connecting threads between your observations. You might notice:

- certain thoughts always lead to specific emotional reactions
- physical tension appears when you think about particular situations
- some patterns have been with you since childhood
- certain beliefs keep limiting your actions

Working with What You Find
As patterns become clear, ask yourself:

- Where did this pattern come from?
- How has it been serving me?
- What would happen if I tried a different approach?
- What support do I need to change this pattern?

Remember, the goal is not to judge or change what you find—at least not at first. It is simply a matter of becoming aware of what has been operating beneath the surface. Often, simply bringing these patterns into consciousness initiates the transformation process.

Tips:

- Start with shorter sessions if 15 minutes feels too long
- Set a regular time each day for this practice
- Be patient - some patterns take time to reveal themselves
- Stay curious rather than judgmental
- Trust that awareness itself is transformative

The beauty of this method is that it is always available to you. Any moment can become an opportunity for awareness. The more you practice observing yourself with kindness and curiosity, the more your unconscious patterns will reveal themselves, allowing you to make different choices.

Remember, you are not trying to fix or change anything yet. You are simply developing the ability to see yourself more clearly. With time and practice, the invisible becomes visible, and what was running on autopilot comes under your conscious control.

The Trigger Tracking Method

This method helps you identify and understand your emotional wounds by carefully observing and documenting your emotional triggers and reactions.

Create Your Trigger Journal
Use a notebook or a note-taking app to track your emotional triggers. Each time you experience a strong emotional reaction, record:

- the situation that triggered you
- your emotional response
- physical sensations in your body (racing heart, stomach knots, etc.)
- the context and circumstances
- your immediate reaction

Look for Common Themes
Review your journal entries regularly to identify patterns:

- Which situations consistently provoke strong reactions?
- What types of words or actions tend to trigger you?
- Are there particular people who frequently

trigger you?
- Do you notice any common physical responses?

Trace the Origins
For each major trigger you identify, explore its history:

- When was the first time you remember feeling this way?
- What past experiences might this trigger connect to?
- Write a 'trigger biography' - the story of how this trigger has shown up throughout your life

Analyse Your Patterns
Look at the bigger picture of your life:

- review your relationship history
- examine your career path
- consider your typical coping mechanisms
- notice recurring themes in different areas of your life

Seek External Perspective

- Ask close friends or family what patterns they notice in your behaviour
- Get feedback on your trigger journal insights

The key to this method is consistency in tracking and a willingness to look honestly at what emerges. Remember, the goal is not to judge yourself but to understand your emotional wounds so you can begin healing them.

Continue practising this method until you begin to see clear connections between your current triggers and past experiences. This understanding is the first step toward healing your emotional baggage.

The Mirror Method

Every person in your life can be a mirror, reflecting back parts of yourself you might not otherwise see. This method helps you use those reflections to uncover and understand your emotional wounds.

Think of the world as one big classroom, with every person you meet being a potential teacher. The way people treat you, react to you, or make you feel is not random - it often connects directly to your own unhealed parts or unacknowledged patterns.

For instance, if you find yourself repeatedly dealing with people who do not respect your boundaries, this may reflect your own difficulty valuing and protecting them. If you keep encountering controlling people, it might be mirroring your own fears about losing control.

Start with Current Relationships
Make a list of the key people in your life right now - the ones who trigger strong emotions in you, whether positive or negative. Include:

- family members
- friends
- colleagues
- current or recent romantic partners

Notice Your Reactions
For each person on your list, write down:

- How they make you feel
- What behaviours of theirs trigger you most
- What you often complain about regarding them
- What you admire or envy about them

Look for Patterns
Review your notes and look for recurring themes. Do you often feel:

- dismissed or unheard?
- controlled or manipulated?
- not good enough?
- responsible for others' feelings?

These patterns usually point directly to your core wounds.

Turn the Mirror Around
This is where it gets interesting and sometimes uncomfortable. For each pattern you have identified, ask yourself:

- How might I be doing this same thing to myself?
- Where else in my life does this pattern show up?
- What old wound might this be touching?
- What am I afraid would happen if this pattern

changed?

Using What You Find
Once you have identified these reflections, you can use them as a map to your healing work. Each difficult person or situation in your life becomes an opportunity to:

- recognise where you need healing
- practice new ways of responding
- build stronger boundaries
- challenge old beliefs

Remember, this is not about blaming yourself for how others treat you. It is about recognising that your external experiences often reflect your internal landscape - and that gives you the power to change them.

Keep a Mirror Journal
Start keeping a journal where you record:

- situations that triggered strong emotions
- people who really got under your skin
- your immediate reaction
- what this might be showing you about yourself

Over time, you will begin to see clear patterns emerge, providing a deeper understanding of your emotional wounds and what requires healing.

This method is not always comfortable - seeing yourself clearly rarely is. However, by recognising that everyone in your life may reveal something about you, you gain powerful insights into your own healing journey. Each difficult person or situation becomes not just a challenge, but an opportunity for growth and self-discovery.

The Heyoka Method

In Native American traditions, particularly among the Lakota people, the Heyoka served as a sacred mirror, deliberately acting in ways that would challenge others to see their blind spots and grow. We can adapt this powerful tradition by working with someone we deeply trust to help us see our emotional patterns more clearly.

Choose Your Heyoka

Find someone who knows you well and whom you trust completely - someone who has seen you at your best and worst, and who cares enough about your growth to be completely honest with you. This could be a close friend, family member, or mentor who is not afraid to challenge you.

Create an Agreement
Sit down with your chosen person and make a clear agreement. Ask them to take on the role of your Heyoka - someone who will deliberately point out your patterns, reactions, and behaviours that you might not see in yourself. This is not about criticism; it is about illumination.

Let Them Trigger You
This is where it gets uncomfortable—and that is exactly the point. Give your Heyoka permission to:

- bring up situations where you overreacted
- point out when you are making excuses
- challenge your stories about why things happen to you
- question your default responses to situations
- mirror back your behaviour in key moments

When they do this, your job is not to defend yourself. Instead, treat every trigger as a treasure map leading to buried emotional gold. The stronger your reaction to what they are showing you, the more important the lesson probably is.

Dig Deeper Together
When something really gets under your skin, pause and explore it together. Ask questions like:

- 'Why do you think this particular thing gets to me so much?'
- 'Have you noticed me reacting this way in other situations?'
- 'What patterns do you see that I might be missing?'

Remember, just like a traditional Heyoka, this process is not about being nice - it is about being truthful. It may feel intensely uncomfortable at times, but that discomfort is often where real growth occurs.

This method works because we often cannot see our own patterns clearly. Just as the Heyoka would act as a reverse mirror for their tribe - doing things backwards to help others see themselves more clearly - your personal Heyoka can help you see the truth about yourself by deliberately triggering your reactions and helping you understand them.

By having someone intentionally point out your triggers and patterns, you can begin to recognise and heal the emotional wounds that have been driving your behaviour. It is a challenging practice, but one that can lead to profound insights and real transformation.

Remember, this is not about judgment or criticism. It is about using the wisdom of an ancient tradition to help you see yourself more clearly and grow beyond your current limitations. The Heyoka were considered sacred for a reason - sometimes the most powerful growth comes when someone cares enough to show us what we have been trying not to see.

The Speak Freely Method

This powerful technique draws inspiration from the Native American tradition of Talking Circles, where each person is given the opportunity to share their thoughts and feelings without interruption, while others listen attentively and deeply.

Choose Your Listening Partner
Find someone you trust - someone who can hold space without trying to fix, solve, or judge. This could be a friend or family member. The key is that you feel safe being completely honest with them.

Set the Space
Find a quiet, private place where you will not be interrupted. Sit comfortably. Turn off your phones and remove other distractions. Take a moment to ground yourselves.

The Speaking Process
For 10 minutes, you speak freely about whatever is on your mind or troubling you. Your partner's job is to:

- Not say anything or interrupt you
- Listen with their full attention
- Maintain gentle eye contact
- Stay completely silent

- Keep track of the time
- Notice not just your words, but your tone, energy, and body language
- Pay attention to patterns or themes that emerge
- Listen for what might be hiding beneath the surface

During your speaking time, you:

- Speak whatever comes to mind without censoring yourself
- Don't worry about making sense or staying on topic
- Allow yourself to follow your train of thought wherever it leads
- Express yourself honestly, including emotions that arise
- Keep talking even if you hit uncomfortable silences

The Reflection
After your 10 minutes are up, your listening partner takes the time to reflect back on what they heard and what they sensed beneath your words. They might notice:

- recurring themes or patterns
- emotional undercurrents
- things you seemed hesitant to say directly
- what lit you up or made you shut down
- where you seemed to avoid or skip over certain topics
- what your body language was saying

They share these observations not as judgments or interpretations, but as gentle reflections of what they noticed. You can then choose to explore these observations further or simply accept them.

Often, when we speak without interruption while someone truly listens, more profound truths begin to emerge. Things we did not even know were troubling us bubble up to the surface. Patterns that were previously invisible become clearer. The simple act of speaking freely in the presence of others can be profoundly healing.

Remember, this is not about getting advice or solutions. It is about creating space for your truth to emerge and having someone bear witness to what lies beneath your everyday thoughts and words.

You can practice this method regularly with your partner, taking turns speaking and listening. Over time, you will likely find that having this dedicated space to talk freely helps you understand yourself more deeply and uncover emotional patterns you may not have been aware of.

The gift of being truly heard, without judgment or interruption, can be transformative. Sometimes the most powerful insights come not from being told what to do, but from having someone hold space while we discover our own truth.

Clarifying Your Emotional Wounds

As you use these methods to uncover your emotional wounds, you may initially find it hard to define them clearly. You might sense there is something there - like feeling around in a dark room - but struggle to put your finger on precisely what it is. This is entirely normal. Emotional wounds can be complex and layered, and their edges are not always clear.

This is where writing becomes a powerful tool. Taking time to describe your wound in writing can help bring it into sharper focus. Think of it like trying to explain an abstract painting to someone - the more you attempt to put it into words, the more details you notice and the clearer the picture becomes.
For example, you might start with a vague sense that you have a wound around 'not being good enough.' Through writing about it, you might discover it is actually more specific than that:

> *Initial attempt at describing the wound:*
> 'I have a wound around not being good enough. It makes me feel bad about myself and work too hard.'
>
> *After spending time clarifying through writing:*
> 'I carry a deep fear that my worth depends entirely on what I achieve. This wound formed during my school years, when I learned that approval and love seemed to come only when I got perfect grades. Now, I've noticed that this wound activates whenever someone gives me feedback - even constructive suggestions feel like evidence that I am failing. It manifests as an intense drive to prove my worth through constant accomplishment, a tendency to abandon projects if I cannot do them perfectly, and a deep fear of being 'found

out' as not actually capable enough. The core belief seems to be that I'm only worthy of love and belonging when I am performing at the highest level.'

See how much clearer and more specific that becomes? By taking time to write it out, you might discover:

- When the wound first formed
- What triggers it
- How it shows itself in your behaviour
- The core beliefs attached to it
- The impact it has on your life

Don't worry about getting it 'right' on the first try. Start with whatever you can articulate, even if it feels messy or unclear. Keep revisiting and refining your description as you gain new insights. You might find that what you initially thought was one wound is actually several related ones, or that what seemed like separate wounds are actually different aspects of the same wound.

Remember, the goal is not to craft a perfect description, but to develop a clearer understanding of what you are working with. This clarity will help guide your healing journey and make it easier to recognise when this wound is influencing your behaviour or reactions.

Step 2: Process and Release Your Emotional Wounds

Now that you can see your emotional wounds clearly, you can begin healing them. This step involves fully acknowledging your emotions (instead of pushing them away), gaining a deep understanding of their origins, extracting the wisdom your struggles have to offer, and examining your experiences from new perspectives.

As you do this, you will naturally start to let go of old pain and outdated beliefs that no longer serve you. Think of it like cleaning out an overstuffed cupboard - you look at each item, decide what it means to you, and choose what to keep and what to release. This is not about forcing anything - it is a natural unfolding that happens when you permit yourself to heal.

Processing emotional wounds requires several key approaches, each playing a vital role in your healing journey. Let us explore each of these approaches in turn.

Feeling What You Have Been Avoiding

You are rushing through your morning routine when suddenly a wave of sadness washes over you. Without thinking, you push it away and dive into your busy day. Sound familiar? Most of us have become experts at dodging our difficult emotions, treating them like unwelcome guests we would rather not face.

But here is what this constant avoidance costs you: Look around, and you will notice that about 95% of people are escaping their emotions. They are operating with low energy, are borderline checked out, and are simply in survival mode. Even people who appear successful on the outside—those with more money or status than you—are often running from themselves. They are carrying invisible backpacks full of unprocessed feelings, and it is exhausting them.

Your protection system has worked overtime to shield you from these difficult emotions, keeping them buried deep within. And while this protective mechanism has served you in the past, it takes tremendous energy to keep emotions suppressed. To truly let go of emotional baggage, it helps to gently turn toward what you have been avoiding.

Understanding Your Emotional Messages

Before diving into feeling your suppressed emotions, it helps to understand that these feelings are not your enemies—they are messengers. Each emotion carries specific information about your needs, boundaries, emotional wounds or experiences. When you can decode these messages, you transform from being overwhelmed by emotions to becoming curious about their wisdom.

Think of emotions like a sophisticated guidance system. Just as physical pain tells you to remove your hand from a hot stove, emotional pain signals what needs attention in your inner world. Here is what your emotions might be trying to tell you:

- *Abandonment* means you feel left behind or discarded by someone important, which can trigger fears of being alone or unlovable.
- *Anger* signals that one of your rules, boundaries, or values has been broken or violated.
- *Anxiety* or worry shows you are anticipating potential problems or threats in the future.
- *Betrayal* indicates someone you trusted has broken that trust.
- *Confusion* reveals that you lack clarity about a situation

or decision.
- *Contempt* suggests you feel superior to or dismissive of someone else.
- *Despair* or hopelessness means you cannot see a positive way forward.
- *Disappointment* or frustration shows that your expectations or hopes have not been met.
- *Disgust* signals that something violates your sense of what is clean, pure, or morally acceptable.
- *Emptiness* or numbness indicates you feel disconnected from your emotions or sense of purpose.
- *Fear* alerts you to a perceived threat to your safety, security, or well-being.
- *Guilt* means you believe you have done something that conflicts with your values or standards.
- *Helplessness* or powerlessness shows you feel unable to influence or change a situation that is important to you.
- *Humiliation* indicates you feel exposed and diminished in front of others.
- *Inadequacy* suggests you believe you are not good enough or capable enough to meet the demands of a situation.
- *Indignation* reveals that you feel moral outrage about injustice or unfairness.
- *Jealousy* or envy means you believe someone else has something you want or need.
- *Loneliness* signals you have an unmet need for connection and belonging.
- *Overwhelm* indicates you feel like you have more to handle than you can cope with.
- *Regret* shows you wish you had made different choices in the past.
- *Rejection* means you feel excluded, unwanted, or not accepted by others.
- *Resentment* or bitterness reveals you are holding onto anger about past hurts and feel that justice has not been served or acknowledgement has not been given.
- *Sadness* indicates you have experienced a loss or separation from someone or something important to you.
- *Shame* suggests you believe there is something fundamentally wrong with who you are.

When you understand that emotions are a form of information, you can approach them with curiosity instead of resistance.

The Practice of Meeting Your Emotions Safely

The process of feeling buried emotions does not have to be overwhelming. Think of it like opening a door just a crack—letting these emotions know it is safe to come out when they are ready. Here is how to create the conditions for gentle emotional exploration:

Prepare Your Space
Find a private, quiet location where you will not be disturbed. Settle into a comfortable position, either sitting or lying down. Remove distractions like phones or devices. This physical safety helps your nervous system relax enough to explore what has been hidden.

Connect Through Your Body
Begin with several slow, deep breaths to centre yourself. Feel where your body makes contact with the chair or floor. Notice any areas of tension or discomfort—your body often reveals emotions before your mind recognises them. Physical sensations are like breadcrumbs leading to buried feelings. That knot in your stomach might be anxiety. The tightness in your throat could be a sign of unexpressed sadness. Shoulder tension often carries stress, while chest heaviness may hold grief.

Gentle Exploration
Bring to mind a situation that has been bothering you—do not analyse it, just hold a general awareness. Notice your body's immediate responses: changes in breathing, muscle tension, throat tightness, chest sensations, stomach reactions. Simply observe without trying to fix or change anything.

Remember: You are not here to solve problems or relive painful experiences. You are simply acknowledging what is present, like a compassionate witness to your own experience.

What to Expect

As you begin this practice, it might feel uncomfortable or even scary at times. That is completely normal - you are challenging patterns that have been with you for years. Think of it like cleaning out a cupboard you have avoided for ages. At first, it may feel overwhelming, but as you work through it day by day, you begin to feel lighter.

This is a gradual process, not a one-time event. Each day, as you practice recognising and releasing these old patterns, you are making space for something new. The emotional baggage that has been weighing you down does not disappear overnight, but slowly, steadily, you will notice it getting easier to carry - until one day, you realise you have set much of it down for good.

Though it may slow you down initially, this process of feeling what you have been avoiding is ultimately the most efficient path to freedom. Do not block the inputs of life—the challenges, the triggers, the difficult emotions—because if you do, your outputs will not be accurate. Your responses to life will be based on avoidance rather than truth.

When you finally sit with your pain and work with your mind, something profound happens. You become truly real, and with that comes genuine confidence—not because you are putting on a show, but because you are no longer fake. Others can sense this authenticity. When you have done the inner work, people sense a difference in you without you even trying.

Managing the Intensity

If you start feeling overwhelmed, that is your signal to pause. Take a step back, focus on your breath, and remind yourself that you are safe in the present moment. This is not about forcing yourself to feel everything at once or pushing through at any cost.

After exploring difficult emotions, do something nurturing for yourself—take a warm bath, go for a walk in nature, or call a supportive friend. These acts of self-care help you integrate what you have experienced.

Sometimes these emotions feel too big to handle alone—and that is perfectly okay. If you find yourself consistently overwhelmed, reaching out for support is not a sign of weakness; it is a sign of wisdom.

Building Your Emotional Strength

Feeling your emotions is like building a muscle—it grows stronger with practice. At first, it might feel uncomfortable or even scary. But with time and patience, you will develop a greater capacity to be with your feelings without being overwhelmed by them.

Each time you turn toward an emotion instead of away from it, you reclaim a piece of your power. You stop letting your past control your present. Your relationships transform as you bring this new genuineness to every interaction.

The next time you notice yourself pushing away an emotion, try this: Close your eyes, take three deep breaths, and simply notice what sensations arise in your body. These are not random feelings—they are valuable messages helping you understand and eventually release your emotional baggage.

By gently feeling what you have been avoiding, you are not just processing old pain—you are clearing the path to become who you truly are.

Deeply Understand Your Emotional Wounds

Understanding your emotional wounds is not just about knowing they exist - it is about truly grasping where they come from, how they affect you, and why they still influence your life today. When you take the time to explore these wounds deeply, you start to see patterns you might have missed before. You begin to understand why certain situations trigger such strong reactions in you, or why you keep finding yourself in similar challenging circumstances.

This deeper understanding is like shining a light into the darker corners of your emotional world. It helps you see that your reactions and behaviours are not random - they are often protective responses to past hurts. By truly understanding your wounds, you gain the power to heal them properly, rather than just covering them with a bandage. This kind of deep exploration might feel uncomfortable at first, but it is through this process that real healing begins. You will find yourself better equipped to make different choices, break old patterns, and create the changes you want in your life.

The Discovery Writing Method

Before we delve into the steps of discovery writing, it is important to understand how this technique differs from everyday journaling. It differs in several important ways. While both involve putting your thoughts on paper, discovery writing takes you on a deeper journey into your inner world. Instead of just recording what is on the surface of your mind, which is what journaling typically does, it helps you access hidden thoughts, feelings, and patterns you might not even know are there. Think of it as being an explorer of your own psyche, venturing into unexplored territory rather than just documenting the familiar landscape.

Unlike the casual nature of regular journaling, where you might write whenever the mood strikes and track how you are feeling over time, discovery writing asks for more structure and commitment from you. You set aside a specific time for it and keep writing continuously during that period. This dedicated practice helps create the mental space needed for deeper insights to emerge.

The main difference lies in the purpose. When you journal, you often record things that have happened or thoughts you are already aware of, process your daily experiences, and note your emotional state. But with discovery writing, your goal is to reveal what lies beneath - to shine a light on parts of yourself that have been hiding in the shadows. You are not just noting down what you already know; you are uncovering new insights and gaining a deeper understanding of yourself. It is like the difference between taking photos of a landscape versus actually digging into the earth to discover what might be buried there. And just like a real treasure hunt, you will often be surprised by what you find - unexpected revelations about yourself that you had not consciously recognised before.

Method:

Getting Started with Discovery Writing
Before you begin, find a quiet, comfortable spot where you will not be interrupted. You will need a pen, a notebook, and at least 20 uninterrupted minutes.

The Power of Handwriting
This practice works best with handwriting rather than digital devices - there is something special about the connection between hand, heart, and mind when you write by hand. When you write by hand, you engage your brain differently than when typing. The physical act of forming letters activates parts of your brain associated with memory and emotional processing, helping you connect more deeply with your emotions. The process creates space for reflection, allowing emotions to surface. Even the way you write - the pressure of your pen, the size of your letters, the spots where you pause - can offer clues about your emotional state. This physical connection makes it easier to identify patterns and understand your emotional responses as you work through your baggage.

Setting Up Your Session
At the top of your page, write down what you want to

explore. Frame it as a simple statement, such as 'I want to understand more about why I feel my worth depends on my achievements.' This helps focus your exploration while keeping it open-ended enough for insights to emerge.

The Writing Process
Set your timer for 20 minutes and start writing whatever comes to mind. Don't worry about making it perfect - spelling, grammar, and even making sense does not matter here. The key is to keep your pen moving continuously across the page. If you get stuck, it is perfectly fine to repeat words or phrases until new thoughts emerge. Let your mind wander where it needs to go. You might start writing about one thing and end up somewhere completely different - that is actually good! Some of the most valuable insights come from these unexpected directions. Even if you feel resistance or want to stop, keep going until the timer goes off. Often, the deepest revelations come just when you think you have nothing left to say.

After Your Session
When your 20 minutes are up, take some time to read over what you have written. You will likely notice patterns or insights you were not aware of while writing, especially in the later parts of your session. These insights might lead you to other areas you want to explore - feel free to do another session focusing on these new discoveries.

Discovery writing is powerful because it helps you bypass your conscious mind and tap into deeper thoughts and feelings you might not normally access. The physical nature of handwriting creates a unique connection between your body, mind, and emotions, allowing you to process your experiences more fully. The combination of continuous writing and the 20-minute minimum creates the mental space needed for insights to surface, while the intimate nature of handwriting helps you feel safe exploring vulnerable territory. Trust the process, even when it feels challenging - you might be surprised by what you discover about yourself.

The Discovery Drawing Method

If you are dyslexic or simply prefer visual expression over written words, you can explore your inner world through drawing instead. This approach utilises shapes, colours, and images rather than words, yet achieves the same profound self-discovery as writing.

Method:

Getting Started with Discovery Drawing
The setup is similar to discovery writing - find a quiet spot with 20 minutes of uninterrupted time. Instead of a pen and notebook, gather coloured pencils, pens or markers and plain paper.

The Power of Drawing
Just as handwriting engages specific parts of your brain, drawing bypasses your logical mind and taps directly into your emotional and intuitive centres. Shapes and colours become your vocabulary - red might emerge for anger, blue for sadness, yellow for hidden joy. The pressure of your pencil, the shapes that appear, and the colours you instinctively choose all offer clues about your emotional state.

The Drawing Process
Like with discovery writing, start by noting what you want to explore at the top of your page. Then set your timer for 20 minutes and begin drawing and making marks. The same rule applies - keep your hand moving continuously. Draw abstract shapes, symbols, spirals, jagged lines, gentle curves, whatever emerges. Don't aim for 'good' art any more than you would aim for perfect spelling in discovery writing. If you get stuck, switch colours or make repetitive marks until something new flows. Layer different colours as feelings shift. Let yourself fill the page with unexpected connections, just as discovery writing might lead you to unexpected insights. If you want to draw something specific but feel you need visual guidance, you can briefly look it up on your phone, though often the most powerful insights come from drawing whatever spontaneously emerges.

After Your Session
When time is up, observe what you have created. Notice dominant colours, repeated symbols, areas of heavy pressure or gentle touch. Turn the page in different ways to gain new perspectives. These visual patterns reveal insights just as written patterns do in discovery writing.

Whether you choose writing or drawing, both methods bypass your conscious mind to access deeper truths. Both create that essential 20-minute container for insights to surface. The only difference is the language - one uses words, the other uses visual expression. Trust whichever process feels most natural to you.

The Digging Deep Method

You can use this approach to gain a deeper understanding of the roots and impact of your emotional wounds. This powerful technique can be used to uncover the core beliefs, habits, and patterns that have developed around your wounds. Understanding these elements really helps you heal.

Method:

The approach involves following a chain of thoughts by repeatedly asking yourself probing questions about a troubling situation or emotion. Start with a surface thought or feeling, then keep asking 'What does this mean to me?' or 'What's the worst part about this?' until you reach the fundamental belief underneath.

As you dig deeper, you will often find that at the root of your emotional wounds lies a basic human need that was not met. These fundamental needs include:

- the need to feel safe (physically, emotionally, and mentally)
- the need to feel loved and accepted
- the need to feel that you matter and have worth
- the need to feel like you belong

For example:

- Surface thought: 'I feel anxious about asking for help'
- What does this mean to me? 'People might think I'm weak'
- What is the worst part about that? 'They might reject me'
- What would that mean? 'I'm not worthy of support'
- Core belief revealed: 'I'm not good enough'
- Unmet need uncovered: The need to feel worthy and that you matter

The key is to keep going until you hit something that feels fundamental - a belief that seems to underlie many of your thoughts and reactions. When you encounter one of these basic unmet needs, you will often experience a strong emotional response or a profound sense of recognition. This emotional response signals that you have reached the root of the wound.

This is how the method can be used to understand the roots of habitual behaviours and life patterns.

Exploring Protective Habits

Start with a behaviour you have noticed, then dig deeper to understand its roots. For example:

- Surface behaviour: 'I always try to do things perfectly'
- What am I trying to achieve? 'I want to avoid making mistakes'
- What am I afraid would happen if I made mistakes? 'People would criticise me'
- What is the worst part about being criticised? 'It would prove I'm not good enough'
- What basic need was not met? 'The need to feel loved and accepted as I am'

Investigating Recurring Patterns

Apply the method to situations that keep showing up in your life:

- Recurring pattern: 'I keep attracting controlling partners'
- What feels familiar about these relationships? 'I always feel like I have to prove myself'
- Why is this pattern comfortable? 'It is what I experienced growing up'
- What am I getting from this pattern? 'At least I know what to expect'
- What unmet need lies beneath? 'The need to feel safe and valued'

As you practice the Digging Deep Method, keep these guidelines in mind:

- Write your thoughts down - seeing them on paper can provide clarity and insight
- Be patient with the process - some beliefs may take time to uncover

- Notice physical sensations as you dig deeper - your body often holds clues to emotional truth
- Look for themes and connections between different situations and reactions

Remember, the goal is not to judge what you discover. Your protection system developed these beliefs and habits for a reason - to keep you safe from perceived threats. By understanding them more deeply, you can begin to recognise which ones still serve you and which ones you are ready to release.

Practice self-compassion as you use this method. Digging deep into emotional wounds takes courage, and each insight you gain is a step toward healing. Take your time with the process, and don't hesitate to seek support if you find yourself overwhelmed by what emerges.

Rethinking & Letting Go

Sometimes, the way we remember our hurts can hinder our ability to heal. Like looking through a clouded lens, our memories of painful moments can keep us stuck in patterns that no longer serve us. But what if we could gently shift our perspective and see these experiences in a new light?

You have come a long way on this journey. You have become aware of your emotional wounds, clarified their origins, allowed yourself to feel what you have been suppressing, and gained a new understanding of your experiences. Now comes one of the most empowering parts of your healing process: using your mind's ability, guided by the wisdom of your soul, to rewrite the stories that have kept you trapped.

To understand how this works, it is important to recognise how your emotional wounds were first formed. When you experienced difficult events in your past, it was not just the events themselves that created lasting pain—it was how your Raven interpreted those experiences and the meanings it assigned to them, and how your Bear and Wolf then acted on those interpretations.

Recall a painful experience from your past. Perhaps you were criticised by a teacher, left out by friends, or felt unsupported during a difficult time. The event itself was just that—an event. But your Raven, trying to make sense of what happened and predict future dangers, began weaving a story:

- 'This means I'm not good enough.'
- 'This proves I'm not safe.'
- 'This shows I don't matter.'
- 'This confirms I don't belong.'

Once your Raven perceived these threats and assigned meanings to them, it immediately alerted your protection system. Your inner Bear got ready to protect you in the moment. Meanwhile, your inner Wolf started planning for the future, creating long-term strategies to ensure you would never experience that kind of pain again.

They were not overreacting—they were doing exactly what they are designed to do: protect you based on the Raven's perception of danger. For years, perhaps decades, this system has been running in the background of your life, keeping the original emotional wound protected but unhealed.

But here is the beautiful truth you have discovered through your healing journey: your Raven—the same part of you that created those limiting interpretations—can now create empowering ones instead. Where it once saw threat and danger, it can learn to see safety and possibility. The mind that is wounded can also be the mind that heals.

Think of rethinking and letting go as slowly adjusting the lens through which you view your past. You are no longer the same person who first experienced that pain. You possess more wisdom, more resources, and a deeper understanding of yourself and the world. Most importantly, you now have conscious awareness of how your mind works and the choice to direct it toward healing rather than protection.

This gentle process might mean:

- noticing when you are being hard on yourself about something that happened
- finding moments of strength you did not see before
- being as kind to yourself as you would be to a dear friend
- letting go of old blame - both of yourself and others
- discovering the wisdom hidden within difficult experiences

When we hold onto our first understanding of painful events, it is like keeping an old wound wrapped in the same bandage. By carefully unwrapping it and looking with fresh eyes, we can:

- release some of the heaviness these memories carry

- build more nurturing relationships with ourselves and others
- find new strength in knowing we can grow from challenges
- create space for more joy and possibility in our lives

Having done the deep work of awareness, clarification, feeling, and understanding, you are now in a position to consciously choose what you want to believe about yourself and your experiences. You can look at those old wounds with new eyes, assign new meanings to past events, and actively release the interpretations that have kept you stuck.

Remember, this is not about dismissing your feelings or pretending the hurt never happened. It is about holding your experiences tenderly while allowing new understanding to emerge. You can honour your past while refusing to let it define your future. Take your time with this process - healing has its own gentle rhythm.
Your Raven is ready to fly in new directions, to gather new evidence, to tell new stories. Your Bear and Wolf can begin to relax their vigilant guard, knowing that you are now strong enough and wise enough to protect yourself in healthier ways.

When you are ready to explore your experiences through a new lens, there are gentle yet powerful practices that can guide you. Four approaches that many people find particularly healing are:

- Finding the Lessons - which helps you discover the hidden gifts in your challenges.
- The Raven Method - which harnesses your mind's natural intelligence to gather new evidence for empowering beliefs.
- Ho'oponopono - an ancient Hawaiian practice of reconciliation and forgiveness that helps restore harmony within yourself and your relationships.
- The Love Letter Method - a profound practice of reconnecting with your true self by allowing your heart and soul to speak directly to you with unconditional love and wisdom.

All four offer different pathways to the same destination: a lighter heart and a fresher perspective on your experiences. Let's examine how you can apply these practices to your own healing journey.

<u>The Finding the Lessons Method</u>

Every emotional wound, no matter how painful, carries within it the seeds of wisdom and growth. When you take the time to understand the deeper meaning behind your struggles, you can transform your pain into powerful life lessons that prevent similar situations from recurring.

Think about some common emotional wounds. If you have experienced betrayal in relationships, the lesson might be about trusting your intuition - those early warning signs you ignored - or about setting clearer boundaries from the start. If you have struggled with burnout from constantly trying to prove your worth through achievement, the wisdom might be about learning to separate your inherent value from your accomplishments. Or if you have dealt with feelings of abandonment, you might discover important lessons about self-reliance and building a stronger internal foundation.

Your painful emotions are actually messengers, each carrying important information. When you feel anger, it often means someone has crossed an important boundary or violated your values. Sadness indicates something meaningful that you have lost or are missing in your life. Fear, when not about immediate physical danger, often highlights areas where you need to build more trust in yourself or develop new capabilities.

Method:

Set aside quiet time with your journal and reflect on a specific emotional wound you have been working on. You may want to review any insights that arose during your discovery writing or other in-depth understanding work.

Ask yourself these questions and write down your answers:

- What patterns do I notice in how this situation developed?
- What needs of mine were not being met?
- What early warning signs did I ignore or miss at the time?
- How was I trying to protect myself?
- What would I do differently now with this new understanding?
- What strength or wisdom did I gain from this experience?

Take time to explore each question fully. Don't rush -

sometimes the deepest insights come after sitting with a question for a while. Write down everything that comes to mind, even if it seems obvious or unimportant at first.

You can also use this process in conversation with someone you trust - sometimes talking through these questions can bring up insights you might miss on your own. Whether you are writing or talking, stay curious and open to whatever emerges. Remember, the aim is not to judge your past actions but to learn from them.

The goal is not to pretend your painful experiences were good or that everything happens for a reason. Rather, it is about choosing to learn and grow from what you have been through. When you extract the lessons from your struggles, you transform your wounds into wisdom that can guide you toward better choices and healthier patterns in the future. This is how you ensure your past pain serves a purpose: use it as a catalyst for positive change in your life.

<u>The Ho'oponopono Method</u>

A very powerful approach to rethinking your emotional wounds is Ho'oponopono. This ancient Hawaiian practice helps you shift your perspective through taking responsibility and expressing four key emotions: remorse, forgiveness, gratitude, and love. What makes this practice so effective is that it addresses both your relationship with yourself and your connection with others involved in the situation.

Method:

Find a quiet space where you will not be disturbed. Have a notebook and pen to hand.

Consider the situation or relationship you wish to heal. Take a few deep breaths to centre yourself.

Write each of these statements in your journal, taking time to explore and feel the emotion behind each one:

'I am sorry...'

- Write what you are sorry for, including how you kept yourself stuck in pain
- If another person was involved, write what you are sorry for in relation to them
- Take responsibility for your part, no matter how

small
- Focus on your power to create change, not on blame

'Please forgive me...'
- Write what you need forgiveness for—from yourself first and foremost
- If applicable, ask forgiveness from others and extend forgiveness to them
- Express what you want to release: resentment, judgment, or pain
- Remember this is about freeing yourself, not condoning harmful behaviour

'Thank you...'
- Find something you are grateful for in this situation, even if it is just the lessons learned
- Thank yourself for your strength and resilience in surviving
- If applicable, thank others for the growth this experience created
- Allow gratitude to transform your perspective

'I love you...'
- First and most importantly, express love to yourself
- If others were involved, extend love to them as well
- Write about finding love even within difficult experiences
- Allow love to flow as a healing force, starting with self-love

Read what you have written, really letting yourself feel each statement. If you think you are in your head, drop to your heart so that you really feel the remorse, the forgiveness, the gratitude and the love.

Keep your writing private if you'd like to - this is primarily for your own healing. You can choose to express these sentiments to others later if you wish.

Remember: Take as much time as you need with each statement. The power lies in fully feeling and meaning each one.

The beauty of Ho'oponopono is that it helps you release old interpretations of painful events and create new meaning, which aids in your healing. By taking responsibility for your experience and consciously choosing remorse, forgiveness, gratitude, and love, you free yourself from the weight of old emotional baggage.

The Love Letter Method

Among the most profound ways to release emotional baggage is to reconnect with your deepest self through writing a love letter from your heart (Deer) and soul (Owl). This practice bypasses your analytical mind (Raven) and protective guardians (Wolf and Bear), allowing your true essence to speak.

When we carry emotional wounds, we often lose connection with our true nature. Our protective systems work overtime, and our analytical mind tries to solve everything; we forget who we really are beneath all the defences and adaptations. This method helps you remember.

Method:

Create a Sacred Space:
Find a quiet place where you will not be disturbed. Light a candle if you wish. Take several deep breaths to centre yourself.

Set Your Intention:
Place one hand over your heart and set the intention to write only from your Deer (emotional wisdom) and Owl (soul wisdom), not from your Raven (analysing mind), Wolf (cautious planner), or Bear (reactive protector).

Begin Your Letter:
At the top of a blank page, write 'Dear [Your Name],' and then allow your heart and soul to express what they most want you to know. Start with: 'What I have always wanted you to know about who you truly are...'

Let Your Deer Speak:
Allow your emotional wisdom to express unconditional love, tenderness, and joy. The Deer's voice might acknowledge:

- how deeply you feel and how beautiful that sensitivity is
- the genuine care you naturally offer others and yourself
- your capacity for joy, wonder, and connection

- the emotional courage you have shown through difficult times

Let Your Owl Speak:
Allow your soul's wisdom to share the larger perspective on your journey and essence. The Owl's voice might remind you of:

- your innate worth, completely separate from achievements or mistakes
- the unique gifts you bring to the world simply by being you
- how all your experiences, even painful ones, have shaped your wisdom
- your connection to something larger than yourself

Close Your Letter:
End with expressions of love and a promise that these wiser parts will stay with you as you continue your journey.

Read Your Letter Aloud:
When you have finished writing, read the letter aloud to yourself, allowing the words to truly sink in. Notice how your body feels as you receive these messages.

This method is powerful because it allows you to access parts of yourself that exist beyond your wounds and protective patterns. Your Owl is the unchanging, wise and powerful aspect of you that is never damaged by painful experiences—it is the essence of who you are.

When you reconnect with this true self, several profound shifts occur:

- You recognise that you have intrinsic worth. When you understand your inherent value, external validation becomes less important. Critical comments or rejection lose their power because your sense of worth comes from within.
- You feel deeply safe within yourself. Connecting with your Owl's wisdom helps you experience a sense of safety that is independent of external circumstances. You begin to trust your ability to weather any storm.
- You know that you matter. Your Deer reminds you of your natural capacity for meaningful connection. This knowledge counters wounds of invisibility or insignificance.
- You experience a sense of belonging. Your Owl helps

you recognise your place in the larger tapestry of life. This deeper belonging transcends social rejection or exclusion.

- You access genuine self-compassion. This practice opens the door to treating yourself with the same kindness you would offer a beloved friend, helping heal wounds of self-criticism.

The beauty of this method is that it does not require you to analyse your wounds or understand their origins. Instead, it directly nourishes the places inside you that have been neglected while you have been busy protecting yourself from pain. By letting your heart and soul speak directly to you, you begin to embody the truth that you are already whole, already worthy, already enough—regardless of what has happened to you or what others have said about you.

This love letter becomes a touchstone you can return to whenever you feel disconnected from your true self. Over time, as you practice receiving love from your own heart and wisdom from your own soul, the emotional baggage that once seemed so heavy begins to fall away naturally, no longer needed on your journey home to yourself.

<u>The Raven Method</u>

In many cultures, the raven is deeply revered as one of the most intelligent creatures—a messenger between worlds, a gatherer of wisdom, and a master storyteller. Ravens are incredibly smart birds that can solve complex problems, use tools, and even learn to imitate human speech. They are natural investigators, always exploring, always collecting, always building something new from what they discover.

In your journey of letting go of limiting beliefs, you can call upon the intelligence of the raven to help you gather new evidence for the beliefs you want to embrace.

Just as a raven flies far and wide to collect twigs, leaves, and shiny objects to build its nest, you are going to send your inner raven out to gather evidence that supports your new, empowering beliefs. Ravens are incredibly thorough—they do not just pick up the first thing they see. They are selective, choosing only what will serve their purpose.

Your Raven knows that your old limiting belief is not true. Like the wise owl that sees clearly in the darkness, there is a part of you that recognises the lies you have been telling yourself. Now it is time to kick out that old nest of false beliefs and fly around gathering new evidence to build something stronger and truer.

Method:

Identify Your Old Story
First, acknowledge what you are ready to release. What story has your mind been telling you? Write it down clearly:

- 'I'm not good enough'
- 'I always mess things up'
- 'People can't be trusted'
- 'I'm not capable of success'

Craft Your New Belief
Decide what you want to believe instead. Your new belief should feel challenging but possible—like a stretch that excites rather than overwhelms you:

- 'I am worthy and capable'
- 'I learn and grow from every experience'
- 'There are trustworthy people in my world'
- 'I have everything I need to succeed'

Send Out Your Raven
Now comes the fun part. Imagine sending your intelligent Raven to gather evidence for your new belief. Ravens are storytellers, and you are giving yours a new story to tell. This brilliant bird will find exactly what you need because that's what they do—they are incredibly resourceful.

Collect Your Evidence
Your Raven will bring back three types of 'twigs and leaves' to build your new nest of beliefs:

Present Evidence: Look for current proof that your new belief is true:

- times when you have succeeded at something
- moments when people have shown you kindness or trust
- instances where you have bounced back from challenges
- examples of your growth and learning

Past Evidence: Send your Raven back through your history:

- childhood moments of courage or creativity
- past relationships that were positive and supportive
- achievements you may have minimised or forgotten
- times when others believed in you

Future Evidence: Your Raven can even scout potential evidence:

- opportunities you could pursue
- skills you could develop
- relationships you could nurture
- goals that feel achievable

Build Your New Nest
Each piece of evidence your Raven brings back becomes a building material for your new belief system. Write them, collect them, celebrate them. Just as a raven carefully weaves each twig into its nest, you are consciously constructing a new foundation for how you see yourself and your possibilities.

Working with Your Raven

- Be patient with the process. Ravens are thorough investigators. Some evidence might take time to appear. Trust that your Raven is working.
- Stay open to unexpected discoveries. Ravens collect unexpected treasures. Be open to evidence appearing in forms you did not anticipate.
- Keep searching every day. Make it a daily practice. Ask your Raven, 'What evidence can you bring me today that supports my new belief?'
- Tell new stories about yourself. Ravens are natural storytellers. Start telling yourself the story of who you are becoming, using the evidence your raven has gathered.

Ravens are incredibly clever —they will find what you are looking for because they know it is there. Trust your inner Raven to uncover evidence supporting your growth. Like any good storyteller, your Raven will help you craft a new narrative about who you are and what you are capable of.

The old nest of limiting beliefs can be dismantled, one twig at a time. And in its place, with the evidence your clever Raven gathers, you can build something magnificent—a new belief system that supports the person you are becoming.

The Ultimate Way to Let Go of Emotional Baggage

While all the methods we have explored for letting go of emotional baggage are valuable, one approach stands above all others: surrender. However, before you misunderstand this word, let us be clear: surrender is not about giving up or becoming passive. It is about letting go of your exhausting need to control everything and trusting in something bigger than yourself.

Many of us hold onto our emotional baggage because we are trying to think our way out of it. We believe that if we just analyse it enough, understand it perfectly, or control it better, we will finally find peace. But here is the truth - some things cannot be figured out with your mind. They can only be released through surrender.

Consider how exhausting it is to constantly try to manage your thoughts, control your emotions, influence others' reactions, and predict future outcomes. It is like trying to hold back the ocean with your bare hands. What if, instead, you could learn to flow with life rather than fight against it?

When you truly surrender, something remarkable happens. You begin to feel supported by life rather than at war with it. You start to trust that there is a wisdom at work that is far greater than your individual mind. This trust allows you to naturally release old patterns and emotional baggage that no longer serve you.

However, here is the interesting part: you cannot force yourself to surrender. It is like trying to make yourself fall asleep - the harder you try, the more it eludes you. Instead, surrender happens gradually as you learn to shift your attention away from your mind's constant chatter and toward a deeper sense of presence.

The beautiful paradox is that when you stop trying to control everything, you actually access a deeper kind of power. It is not the power of force or manipulation, but the power of alignment with life itself. This alignment creates the space for your emotional baggage to fall away naturally.

Remember, your emotional baggage is not something you have to figure out on your own. By practising surrender, you open the door to greater wisdom that helps you release what no longer serves you. Sometimes the bravest thing you can do is simply let go and trust.

A Suggested Combination of Methods

If you are doing Head-to-Heart Healing for yourself, these three methods work well together:

- Start with the Introspection Method to identify your emotional wounds through gentle self-exploration, asking yourself what you are trying to protect and when you have felt this way before.
- Then move to Discovery Writing, setting aside 20 uninterrupted minutes to write continuously by hand, allowing deeper insights to emerge as you bypass your conscious mind.
- Finally, practice Ho'oponopono to shift your perspective through the four healing statements: 'I'm sorry,' 'Please forgive me,' 'Thank you,' and 'I love you.'

This combination creates a natural progression from recognition to understanding to release, guiding you through the complete process of moving emotional wounds from your head to your heart, where true healing can occur.

Keeping It Going Day by Day

Healing from emotional baggage is not a one-and-done process - it is a journey that unfolds day by day. While we cannot erase the past, we can develop daily practices that help us heal old wounds and prevent new ones from forming. Let us explore powerful ways to continue your healing journey.

The Evening Check-In

You know that feeling when something happens and it just does not sit right with you? Maybe someone said something that hurt, or you went through a stressful situation that left you feeling off-balance. These moments, if left unaddressed, can turn into emotional baggage.

Here is a simple practice to catch these forming wounds before they become permanent residents in your emotional backpack.

> At the end of each day, take a few quiet moments to reflect. Scan your day for any moments that still feel uncomfortable or heavy. These are potential wounds in the making.

For each moment you identify, ask yourself:

- What basic need was not met here? (Safety? Love? Belonging? Respect?)
- What meaning am I giving this event?
- How is my protection system trying to handle this?

Now, consciously choose how you want to hold this experience:

- Can you see it from another perspective?
- What would be a more empowering way to think about what happened?
- How might you respond differently if a similar situation occurs?

Think of it like cleaning a cut - if you tend to it right away, it is much less likely to leave a scar. The same goes for emotional wounds. By addressing them on the day they occur, you prevent new layers of emotional baggage from forming.

Finding Support in a Talking Circle

While individual practices, such as evening check-ins, are powerful, sometimes we need the support of others on our healing journey. A Talking Circle, an ancient Native American practice, creates a sacred space where everyone is equal and healing emerges naturally through sharing and being truly heard.

Setting Up Your Circle

Gather Your Group

- Invite 4-8 trusted people interested in emotional healing
- Keep it small to maintain intimacy and allow everyone time to share
- Meet regularly to build trust and connection

Create Your Space

- Choose a quiet, comfortable location
- Arrange seats in a circle where everyone can see each other
- Add meaningful objects or candles to create an atmosphere
- Select a special item to use as your talking piece - perhaps a smooth stone, feather, shell, or small wooden heart that feels comfortable to hold and

meaningful

Core Guidelines

- Only the person holding the talking piece speaks
- Everyone else listens deeply without planning responses
- No advice unless specifically requested
- What is shared stays in the circle
- Honour both speech and silence

Running Your Circle

Opening

- Begin with a moment of silence
- Set an intention for the gathering
- Choose a theme if desired

Sharing Rounds

- Pass the talking piece around
- Each person shares from the heart
- Take time for multiple rounds if needed

Closing

- End with reflection and acknowledgement
- Express gratitude for the sharing

Remember, this is not therapy - it is a space where healing happens naturally through being witnessed and witnessing others with compassion. Through regular participation, you will likely find that both giving and receiving support become a powerful catalyst for your emotional healing.

Let go of any pressure to 'fix' each other. Simply create the space, hold it with respect, and trust in the healing power of being truly heard.

The Nature of Your Healing Journey

As you embark on releasing your emotional baggage, it is important to understand the true nature of this process. Healing is not like following a recipe or assembling furniture with step-by-step instructions. It is something far more organic, mysterious, and—yes—messy.

Embracing the Messy Path

Your healing journey will not be a linear process. There is no clean progression from 'broken' to 'fixed,' no straight line from pain to peace. Growth happens in spirals, waves, and unexpected leaps. You might feel like you are making tremendous progress one day, only to find yourself triggered by something small the next. This is not failure—this is how real healing unfolds.

We live in a culture that promises quick fixes and three-step solutions. Part of you might hope that by following the right techniques or gaining the right insights, you can fast-track your healing or somehow bypass the messy middle altogether. But true transformation does not work that way. It requires surrendering to an unknown process that your mind cannot fully control or predict.

The Undoing, Not the Doing

Real healing is more about undoing than doing. While the techniques and practices in this chapter are valuable tools, the deeper work occurs through an organic unravelling. You are not building yourself into someone new—you are peeling away the layers that have covered the real you.

This undoing requires a different kind of effort than you are accustomed to. It is not the forceful, wilful effort you use to achieve external goals. Instead, it is a gentler allowing, a willingness to let your inner wisdom guide the process even when you cannot see where it is leading.

Sacred Tension and Paradox

As you heal, you will likely experience what feels like contradictory forces within you. Part of you wants to grow and heal, while another part resists change and clings to familiar patterns. Part of you seeks control, while another part knows you must surrender. This tension is not a problem to be solved—it is a sacred aspect of being human.

You might find yourself holding seemingly opposite truths at the same time: You are doing your best, and you could do better. You are not broken, and you need healing. You can make your own choices, but some things are beyond your control. Learning to hold these paradoxes with grace is part of the wisdom that emerges through healing.

Trust the Process

Your rational mind wants to understand exactly how healing works, to map out the journey ahead. But the deepest healing happens in the space beyond mental understanding. It emerges from a knowing that lives in your body, your heart, your soul—a wisdom that does not speak in the loud voice of the mind but whispers through intuition and feeling.

This does not mean abandoning all effort or becoming passive. Rather, it means learning to discern between the striving that comes from fear and the action that flows from deeper wisdom. Sometimes healing requires you to do something; sometimes it requires you to stop doing and simply be present with what is.

You Are Not Broken

Despite what your inner critic might tell you, despite the messages you may have received from others, you are not broken. You are a human being having a human experience, complete with wounds, shadows, and imperfections. Your emotional baggage is not evidence of your defectiveness—it is proof of your sensitivity, your capacity to feel, and your courage in persevering despite difficult experiences.

The voice that tells you that you are fundamentally flawed is not your truth. Beneath that voice is a quieter knowing that recognises your inherent wholeness, your basic goodness, your enough-ness exactly as you are.

Finding Your Support

While the deepest healing happens within you, it doesn't always occur in isolation. Seek out communities, teachers, and resources that point you toward your own inner wisdom rather than promising to fix you from the outside. The most helpful support comes from those who see your wholeness even when you cannot see it yourself.

Books, courses, and techniques can be valuable allies on your journey, but they are not the source of your healing. They are more like gentle reminders that point you back to the wisdom that already lives within you.

The Quiet Revolution

As you heal and release your emotional baggage, you might expect dramatic revelations or obvious transformations. However, often the deepest shifts occur quietly. You may simply notice that you react differently to stress, that old triggers no longer grip you as they used to, and that you have more space between feeling and reacting.

This is not about becoming someone else or transcending your humanity. It is about becoming more fully yourself—more present, more authentic, more at peace with the beautiful, messy, paradoxical experience of being alive.

Remember: Your healing journey is yours alone. Trust the process, be patient with yourself, and know that every step—even the ones that feel like steps backwards—is moving you toward greater freedom and wholeness.

Finding Home Within Yourself

After doing the work to recognise, process, and release your emotional wounds, something remarkable happens. The very things you have been seeking from the outside world - safety, love, acceptance, and belonging - begin to emerge from within you.

For most of your life, you may have been looking outward for these fundamental needs. You sought safety in your surroundings, love from others, validation that you matter, and communities where you might belong. There is nothing wrong with wanting these things - they are basic human needs. But when you heal your emotional baggage, you discover that the most reliable source of these feelings is not external at all.

When you have done your inner work, safety transforms from something you need from your environment into something you carry with you. That constant background anxiety, the feeling that things could fall apart at any moment, begins to fade. You develop a deep trust in your ability to handle whatever comes your way. You have faced your deepest fears in your healing journey and survived. What could be scarier than that? This does not mean bad things will not happen - they will. But you know in your bones that you can weather any storm.

Love shifts from something you chase to something you embody. All those years of seeking love to fill the emptiness inside give way to a profound sense of self-compassion. You have learned to sit with your wounded parts, to listen to them with kindness, to hold space for your own pain. This is love in its purest form. And from this wellspring of self-love, you become capable of giving and receiving love more authentically than ever before. You no longer need others to make you feel worthy of love - you already know that you are.

The need to matter and be accepted transforms, too. Remember how you changed yourself to fit in? How you hid parts of yourself in order to gain approval? After healing, you realise that others' opinions do not determine your worth. You matter simply because you exist. There is a profound peace in this recognition - you no longer need to prove your value or earn your place. Your existence itself is enough, and this knowledge radiates from within, changing how you move through the world.

And belonging? This might be the most beautiful transformation of all. After healing, you discover that you belong to yourself first. That sense of being an outsider, of never quite fitting in, dissolves as you recognise that you are part of something much larger—the shared human experience with all its messiness and beauty. You belong to life itself, and this connection can never be taken from you.

This inner sense of home does not mean you stop valuing relationships or community. Quite the opposite. When you are no longer desperately seeking external validation to fulfil these core needs, your connections with others become more genuine and nourishing. You choose relationships because they bring joy and growth, not because you need them to feel complete. The beauty of discovering these feelings within yourself lies in their consistency. External sources of safety, love, acceptance, and belonging can shift or disappear. Jobs end, relationships change, communities evolve. But when these feelings emerge from within, they become your constant companions, available to you even in your darkest moments.

This is the ultimate freedom that comes from letting go of your emotional baggage. You no longer walk through life feeling like something essential is missing or that you are at the mercy of circumstances and other people for your emotional well-being. You carry your home within you, complete with all the safety, love, acceptance, and belonging you could ever need.

And from this place of wholeness, you can truly begin to create the life you want - not from a place of lack or need, but from a place of abundance and choice. This is not just healing; this is transformation. This is coming home to yourself.

EMBRACE REAL LOVE

Ancient Wisdom & Universal Laws:

- *'Love is patient, love is kind,' taught ancient wisdom, revealing what the Law of Attraction confirms: love is not merely an emotion but the fundamental creative force of existence.*
- *The Buddhist metta practice begins with self-compassion because, as the Law of Correspondence shows, the love you cultivate within becomes the love you experience without. This timeless understanding illuminates the path of rebecoming: when you shift from fear-based conditional attachment to heart-centred unconditional love, you align with the universe's most transformative power.*

Love is the most powerful force in the Universe. It is not just a fleeting emotion or a romanticised sentiment, but a fundamental principle woven into the very fabric of existence. When understood and embraced, it has the power to transform not only our own lives but the world around us.

In the previous chapters, we have explored the process of letting go of old stories and releasing emotional baggage. But what fills the space when we clear away these limitations? The answer is love—real, heart-based love that flows naturally when we remove the blocks created by fear and conditioning. This chapter will guide you from understanding what real love truly is to living from this transformative power every day.

Understanding Real Love

What Is Real Love?

The truth is that real love is not something you think—it is something you feel deep in your heart. It is not about logic or reasons. It is not even an emotion but a 'state of being'. It is a vibration that resonates through your entire being. When you are in a state of real love, you are not just loving someone or something; you are being love itself.

What we often refer to as love is actually mind-based or fear-based, rather than heart-based. This mind-based love is conditional, calculated, and often driven by what we can get rather than what we can give. It is rooted in attachment, possession, and the fear of loss. It is the kind of love that comes with terms and conditions, expectations and requirements.
In contrast, heart-based love is:

- unconditional - loving without requirements or expectations
- accepting - embracing both the light and shadow in yourself and others
- free from fear - not worried about loss or rejection
- independent - it comes from within, not dependent on external factors
- whole and complete - it does not need anything to be fulfilled

Heart-based love does not ask, 'What will I get?' Instead, it naturally wonders, 'What can I give?' Not from a sense of sacrifice or martyrdom, but from a genuine overflow of love that already exists within you.

The Core Emotions of Love and Fear

At the deepest level, there are only two core emotions: love and fear. Everything else stems from these two. This understanding can revolutionise how we perceive our emotional experiences and navigate life's challenges.
Love encompasses all expansive emotions:

- joy and celebration
- peace and contentment
- enthusiasm and passion
- compassion and empathy
- gratitude and appreciation

These emotions expand our consciousness, open our hearts, and connect us with others and the world around us. When we operate from love, we see possibilities, feel connected, and naturally want to contribute.

Fear, on the other hand, is at the root of contractive emotions:

- anger and resentment
- jealousy and envy
- anxiety and worry
- hatred and contempt
- shame and guilt

These emotions contract our awareness, close us off from others, and often lead to destructive behaviours. When we operate from fear, we perceive threats, feel isolated, and instinctively move into a protective mode.
By viewing our emotional landscape through this lens of love

versus fear, we gain a powerful tool for personal transformation. Every moment offers us a choice: Will we respond from love or react from fear? This simple question can guide us toward more conscious, heart-centred living.

Understanding Love's Forms

The Many Faces of Love

Love expresses itself in countless ways throughout our lives, each form offering its own gifts and lessons:

- Self-love: The foundation for all other forms of love. Without a loving relationship with yourself, other forms of love become distorted by neediness or fear.
- Familial love: The bond between parents and children, siblings, and extended family. This love often teaches us about the importance of unconditional acceptance and loyalty.
- Friendship love: The deep connection and affection we feel for close friends. This love exemplifies the joy of a chosen family and mutual support.
- Romantic love: The passionate and intimate love between partners. While often idealised, at its best, it combines friendship, passion, and deep commitment.
- Compassionate love: The love we feel for all of humanity, often expressed through kindness and service. This love connects us to our shared humanity.
- Love for nature: The awe and appreciation we feel for the natural world. This love reminds us of our place in the larger web of life.
- Love for animals: The special bond we share with our animal companions. This love teaches us about loyalty, presence, and unconditional acceptance.
- Love for passions: The joy and fulfilment we derive from activities or work we are passionate about. This love connects us to our purpose and creativity.

The Binary Nature of Love

One of the most liberating truths about love is that it is not on a scale where you can love someone 'more' or 'less.' Love is binary—it is either there or it is not. This understanding frees you from the societal pressure to constantly prove or measure your love.

You do not partially love your child or somewhat love your best friend. The essence of love is whole. What can fluctuate, though, are emotions, attachment, and external expressions—not love itself.

When someone says, 'I love you more today than yesterday,' what they are really saying is that their feelings of affection or attachment have increased. But true love—the heart-based kind—remains constant. It is a steady presence that remains constant, unaffected by circumstance.

This binary nature means:

- you either choose love or you choose fear
- love does not need to be earned or proven
- love is not diminished by distance or time
- love does not require reciprocation to exist

Understanding this frees you from love's common distortions—jealousy, possessiveness, and the constant need for validation. When you know love is complete in itself, you can give it freely without depleting yourself.

Cultivating Self-Love

Understanding Self-Love

At the heart of all expressions of love is the most fundamental relationship you will ever have—your relationship with yourself. Self-love is not about indulging your every whim or posting inspirational quotes on social media. It is not narcissism or self-absorption. At its core, self-love means loving all that you are and treating yourself with the same kindness, respect, and care you would offer to someone you deeply value.

Think of someone you love unconditionally—perhaps a child, a best friend, or a partner. How do you treat them? You likely:

- speak to them with kindness, even when pointing out mistakes
- forgive them when they mess up
- make sure their basic needs are met
- celebrate their successes, no matter how small
- stand up for them when others treat them poorly
- listen to them when they are struggling

Self-love means doing these same things for yourself. It means recognising your inherent worth beyond your achievements, appearance, or what you do for others. It means understanding that you deserve kindness and care simply because you exist.

The Inner Relationship

The relationship you have with yourself is the most important one you will ever have. It is also the longest—you are with yourself from birth until death. Yet most of us put more effort into our relationships with others than into this fundamental inner connection.

Your Inner Dialogue

Pay attention to how you speak to yourself throughout the day. Is your inner voice kind and supportive, or harsh and critical? Many of us have internalised an inner critic that constantly points out our flaws, compares us to others, and tells us we are not enough.

To transform this relationship, start by simply noticing your self-talk. When you catch yourself being harsh, pause and ask: 'Would I say this to someone I love?' If not, try rephrasing your thoughts with kindness. For example, instead of 'I'm so stupid for making that mistake,' try 'That mistake doesn't define me. I'm learning and growing.'

Building Self-Trust

Many of us have learned not to trust our own judgment. We override our intuition, break promises to ourselves, and ignore our own needs and boundaries. Rebuilding this trust happens through small, consistent actions:

- make and keep small promises to yourself
- honour your feelings rather than dismissing them
- acknowledge when you have let yourself down, and recommit without harsh judgment
- celebrate when you follow through on commitments to yourself

Each time you keep a promise to yourself, you are making a deposit of trust into your relationship with yourself. Over time, these deposits create a solid foundation of self-trust.

Connecting With Your Intuition

Your body and intuition are constantly sending you signals about what you need and what is right for you. Your intuition might speak through:

- physical sensations: tension, relaxation, energy shifts
- emotional responses: sudden anxiety, unexpected joy, inexplicable discomfort
- quiet inner knowing: that still, small voice that simply knows
- dreams and creative inspirations

Start small by checking in with yourself before making decisions. Ask yourself: 'How does this feel in my body? What's my intuition saying?' With practice, you will learn to distinguish between your intuitive wisdom and fear-based thoughts.

Practical Ways of Cultivating Self-Love

Daily Self-Compassion Practices

Self-compassion means treating yourself with the same kindness you would offer a good friend. Try these simple practices:

- Place your hand on your heart when you are struggling and say, 'This is difficult right now. I'm doing my best.'
- Write yourself a compassionate letter from the perspective of a loving friend
- Take three deep breaths when you notice you are being hard on yourself
- Create a self-compassion phrase to use in difficult moments, like 'I'm human and imperfect, just like everyone else'

Overcoming the Inner Critic

Your inner critic likely developed as a misguided attempt to keep you safe or motivate you. Remember from our earlier discussions about emotional baggage—this critic is actually your protection system speaking. It is the Bear and Wolf we talked about, standing guard to prevent you from experiencing pain again.

As you heal your emotional wounds through the work we have been exploring, your inner critic will naturally have less and less to say. The Bear and Wolf will finally rest when they realise the danger has passed. But in the meantime, while you are still in the healing process, here is how to work with your protective inner critic:

- Name your critic to create some distance (e.g., 'There goes my perfectionist again' or 'Hello, protective bear')
- Get curious about its concerns: 'What are you afraid will happen if I'm not perfect?' Remember, it is trying to protect you from a wound that has not fully healed yet
- Thank it for trying to protect you, then gently correct its outdated information: 'Thank you for keeping me safe all these years, but I'm stronger now'
- Replace criticism with constructive feedback that acknowledges both strengths and areas for growth

Remember that motivation through encouragement is more effective and sustainable than motivation through criticism. As your wounds heal and you develop more self-love, you will notice your inner critic's voice becoming quieter, less urgent, and eventually transforming into a supportive inner guide rather than a harsh protector.

Embracing Imperfection

Perfectionism is the enemy of self-love. It sets an impossible standard and makes your worth conditional on achievement. Practice allowing yourself to be imperfect by:

- sharing work that is 'good enough' rather than perfect
- laughing at your mistakes instead of berating yourself
- focusing on progress rather than perfection
- taking risks even when success is not guaranteed
- appreciating your growth journey rather than fixating on the destination

Real Love in Relationships

Recognising Real Love in Action

Real love goes much deeper than surface-level attractions or societal expectations. It is about who someone is at their core, not what they look like or what they have.

In action, real love manifests as:

- supporting your partner's dreams, even if they differ from your own
- offering forgiveness and understanding when mistakes are made
- celebrating each other's successes without jealousy
- being present and attentive during difficult times
- respecting boundaries and individual needs

- encouraging personal growth and independence

What real love feels like:

- there is a sense of spaciousness and freedom, not constriction or anxiety
- you feel peaceful in their presence, not constantly on edge or performing
- you can be completely yourself, without pretence or fear
- you want what is best for them, even if it does not benefit you
- you see them clearly, with all their flaws and strengths, and love the whole person
- your love does not demand anything from them to be maintained

Conditional Versus Unconditional Love

Understanding the distinction between conditional and unconditional love is essential for fostering healthy relationships.

Conditional love says:

- 'I'll love you if...'
- 'I'll love you when...'
- 'I'll love you as long as...'

This love is based on performance, appearance, or behaviour. It is given or withdrawn based on whether someone meets our expectations. This type of love creates anxiety, performance pressure, and a constant fear of not being enough.

Unconditional love says:

- 'I love you no matter what.'
- 'I love you even when...'
- 'I love you regardless...'

This love accepts people for who they are, flaws and all. It does not mean accepting harmful behaviour—you can love someone unconditionally while still maintaining healthy boundaries. It means your love is not contingent on their perfection.

It is crucial to recognise when what is being called 'love' is actually rooted in fear or manipulation. Red flags to watch for:

- attempts to control or change the other person

- jealousy disguised as care
- using guilt or shame to influence behaviour
- withholding affection as punishment
- constant criticism or lack of respect for boundaries

Remember, real love creates a safe space. It builds trust and lifts you up; it does not tear you down or make you feel small.

Boundaries are the limits you set that protect your physical, emotional, and mental well-being. They are not about controlling others; they are about taking responsibility for your own needs and experiences.

Setting healthy boundaries might include:

- saying no to additional commitments when you are already stretched thin
- limiting time with people who drain your energy
- communicating clearly about what you can and cannot do
- removing yourself from situations that feel harmful
- defining what kind of communication and behaviour you will accept

Every boundary you set is a message to yourself that your needs and well-being matter. Boundaries are actually an expression of love—both self-love and love for others—because they create the conditions for healthy, sustainable relationships.

Living from Love

The Power of Choosing Love

The most liberating truth about love is that it is always a choice. No matter what someone else does or does not do, you always have the power to choose a loving response—even if that response is creating healthy boundaries or walking away. Choosing love does not mean accepting mistreatment or staying in unhealthy situations. Sometimes the most loving choice—for both yourself and the other person—is to end a relationship. But you can do so from a place of love rather than resentment or revenge.

When you choose heart-based love, you are not dependent on others to love you back in order to feel complete. Your love is not contingent on their response. This frees you from the endless cycle of seeking validation and affirmation from outside yourself.

A New Definition of Love

Perhaps it is time to redefine what we mean by love. Not as:

- a feeling that comes and goes
- a transaction or bargain
- something we fall into and out of

But as:

- our essential nature
- our true state of being when we remove all blocks created by fear
- the fundamental creative force of existence

Love is not something you do—it is something you are. And when you begin to recognise and live from this truth, everything changes. Your relationships transform, your experience of life deepens, and you discover that the love you have been seeking outside yourself has been within you all along.

Letting go of emotional baggage related to love means that fear-based love is no longer what we give and receive. When we release the past hurts, disappointments, and traumas that have shaped our understanding of love, we create space for something more genuine to emerge. With our emotional baggage set down, we can finally experience and offer heart-based love—the kind that flows freely without demands or conditions.

What Dogs Teach Us About Love

Sometimes the most profound teachers of love come on four legs, wagging their tails, and asking for nothing more than your presence. Dogs, in their beautiful simplicity, embody the very essence of real love that we humans often complicate or forget how to give and receive.

Watch a dog greet their beloved human after any absence—whether it has been five minutes or five hours. Their entire being lights up with pure joy. There is no holding back, no playing it cool, no calculating whether they should show their excitement. They give their whole heart, completely and without reservation.
A dog does not love you because of what you accomplish, how you look, or what you provide. They love you because you exist.

They love you when you are in your pyjamas with your hair messy. They love you even when you make mistakes. They love you when you are sad, angry, or confused. Their love is not conditional on your performance or your mood—it simply is.

Dogs do not play emotional games. They do not withhold affection to make a point. They do not love you less when they are upset with you. They do not make you guess how they feel or punish you with silence. Real love should never leave you guessing. It should be clear, consistent, and reliable.

Perhaps most beautifully, a dog's love feels safe. You never worry that your dog will suddenly decide you are not worth loving. You never fear that one mistake will cost you their affection. This safety—this deep knowing that you are loved no matter what—is what allows true intimacy to flourish.

You deserve the kind of love dogs give—wholehearted, consistent, and safe. You deserve someone who chooses you not just once, but every day. And perhaps most importantly, you deserve to give this kind of love to yourself.

Moving Forward with Love

Love is indeed the most powerful force in the universe. By embracing a deeper understanding of real love—one that is unconditional, accepting, and liberating—we can transform our relationships, our lives, and our world.

As you move forward, remember:

- start with self-love; it is the foundation for all other love
- choose love over fear in each moment
- real love feels safe, consistent, and freeing
- you are worthy of unconditional love simply because you exist

The journey toward real love starts with loving yourself unconditionally. From that solid foundation, you can extend genuine love to others and receive it in return. This is not just a nice idea—it is the key to living a life of authentic connection, inner peace, and true fulfilment.

After all, as our four-legged teachers have been showing us all along, love does not have to be complicated. It can be as simple as showing up with your whole heart, again and again, without conditions or games. Perhaps it is time we finally listened to their wisdom about what real love truly looks like.

Two of history's most profound teachers on love—Rumi, the 13th-century Sufi mystic whose poetry has touched millions, and Osho, the modern spiritual teacher who dedicated his life to awakening consciousness—share a common understanding. As Rumi reminds us, "Your task is not to seek love, but merely to seek and find all the barriers within yourself that you have built against it." The love you have been searching for has been within you all along. Osho echoes this truth: "Love is a state of being; one is not in love, one is love." When you remove the blocks of fear and conditioning, love flows naturally—not as something you do, but as something you are. "Love is the bridge between you and everything," Rumi wrote—including the bridge back to your own authentic self.

PRACTICE SELF-CARE

Ancient Wisdom & Universal Laws:

- *The Buddhist metta practice begins with the self for a reason: as the Law of Correspondence reveals through the Hermetic principle 'as above, so below; as within, so without,' the love you cultivate within creates your experience without. This ancient wisdom teaches that your inner landscape is mirrored in your outer reality—self-care is not selfish but essential for the whole.*

- *Ayurvedic wisdom teaches that true self-care honours your unique constitution—what nurtures one may deplete another—while the Law of Rhythm shows that respecting your natural cycles of rest and activity restores your vital energy. This ancient understanding illuminates the path of rebecoming: when you tend to yourself first, you create not depletion but a wellspring from which all your relationships and creations can flourish.*

In many ways, self-care is a form of self-love in action. It is a practical application of the understanding that you deserve to be cared for and that your well-being matters.

The Five Dimensions of Self-Care

Physical Self-Care

<u>Body Wisdom</u>

Your body continuously communicates its needs through sensations, energy levels, and subtle signals. Most of us have learned to override these messages, pushing through fatigue, ignoring hunger, or dismissing discomfort. Reconnecting with your body's wisdom starts with simply paying attention.

Try regular body scans where you mentally travel from head to toe, noticing sensations without judgment. With practice, you will become more attuned to your body's signals before they escalate into pain or illness.

<u>Constitutional Awareness</u>

Ayurveda teaches that each person has a unique constitution or dosha—a combination of elemental energies that influence physical, mental, and emotional tendencies. Understanding your predominant dosha helps you recognise what keeps you in balance and what throws you off centre.

The three primary doshas are:

- *Vata* (air and space): Creative, quick, and changeable; prone to anxiety when unbalanced.
- *Pitta* (fire and water): Focused, ambitious, and intense; prone to irritability when unbalanced.
- *Kapha* (earth and water): Steady, nurturing, and calm; prone to lethargy when unbalanced.

Most people are a combination of doshas, with one or two being predominant. Online quizzes or consultations with Ayurvedic practitioners can help you determine your unique constitution.

Nourishment

Food is more than fuel—it is information for your body, affecting not just physical health but mental and emotional wellbeing. Different body types benefit from different foods:

- vata types often thrive on warm, moist, grounding foods
- pitta types generally do well with cooling, sweet, and bitter foods
- kapha types typically benefit from light, dry, and spicy foods

Beyond what you eat, how you eat matters. Eating mindfully in a calm environment improves digestion and nutrient absorption. Notice how different foods affect your energy, mood, and digestion, and adjust your diet accordingly.

Movement That Honours Your Body

Exercise is not about punishing your body or forcing it into submission. Movement should bring joy and vitality while respecting your unique constitution:

- Vata types often benefit from gentle, grounding practices such as yoga or walking.
- Pitta types may thrive with moderate, cooling activities like swimming or cycling.
- Kapha types typically need more vigorous, stimulating exercise, such as dancing or hiking.

The key is finding movement that feels good to your body. Exercise until you feel energised, not exhausted. Pay attention to timing too—morning exercise often provides the most benefit, particularly between 6:00 a.m. and 10:00 a.m., when your energy naturally peaks.

Rest and Recovery

In our busy world, rest often gets sacrificed. Yet proper rest is essential for health and balance. Create a sleep environment that promotes relaxation—cool, dark, and quiet. Develop a calming bedtime routine that might include gentle stretching, meditation, or reading.

Rest is not just about sleep. It also includes:

- short breaks throughout your workday
- days off to recharge
- activities that feel restorative rather than depleting
- periods of doing nothing, allowing your mind and body to simply be

Emotional Self-Care

Emotions are information, not inconveniences to be suppressed or overcome. Emotional self-care begins with allowing yourself to feel what you feel without judgment or rushing to 'fix' it.

Create a regular time to check in with your emotional state. You might journal, talk with a trusted friend, or simply sit quietly and notice what is present. The simple act of acknowledging your feelings often allows them to move through you more easily.

Healthy Emotional Expression

Finding appropriate ways to express emotions prevents them from becoming stuck or manifesting as physical symptoms. This might include:

- journaling or creative expression for processing emotions
- physical movement to release emotional energy
- tears when you need to cry
- voicing frustrations in constructive ways
- celebration and laughter for positive emotions

Different emotions may need different forms of expression. Experiment to find what works for you.

Working With Difficult Feelings

It is important to distinguish between processing everyday emotions and healing deeper emotional wounds. In the 'Let Go of Your Emotional Baggage' chapter, we explored how to work with significant traumas and long-standing emotional wounds that have shaped your identity and behaviours over time. Here, we focus on how to handle the emotions that arise in daily life.

Instead of avoiding challenging emotions, work with them:

- name the emotion specifically ('I'm feeling disappointed about not getting that promotion')
- locate it in your body and notice its qualities (sensation, temperature, movement)
- breathe into that area with compassion
- ask what this emotion needs or is trying to tell you
- take appropriate action based on its message

Remember that emotions are temporary states, not permanent identities. You are not your fear or anger—you are the awareness that experiences these passing emotions. By developing the skill of working with everyday emotions, you will become more resilient and less likely to suppress feelings that could later develop into emotional baggage.

Cultivating Positive Emotional States

While it is important to make space for difficult emotions, you can also actively cultivate positive emotional states through:

- gratitude practices like keeping a thank-you journal
- intentionally noticing moments of joy throughout your day
- savouring pleasant experiences by fully engaging your senses
- acts of kindness that generate feelings of connection and warmth
- reminiscing about positive memories

Mental Self-Care

Thought Awareness

Your mind generates thousands of thoughts daily, but you do not have to believe or act on all of them. Mental self-care begins with becoming aware of your thought patterns without judgment.

Notice recurring thoughts or beliefs that create suffering, such as 'I should be further along in life' or 'I'm not good enough.' Question these thoughts rather than accepting them as truth. Ask yourself: 'Is this actually true? Is there evidence contradicting this belief? What would be a more balanced perspective?'

Information Boundaries

In today's world, we are constantly bombarded with information—much of it negative, sensationalised, or designed to trigger strong emotional responses. Mental self-care includes creating healthy boundaries around information consumption:

- limit news and social media to specific times
- curate feeds to include uplifting and meaningful content
- take regular digital detoxes
- be selective about what books, podcasts, and shows you consume

Intellectual Stimulation

Your mind needs both rest and a healthy challenge. Engage in activities that stimulate your intellect and creativity:

- learning new skills or subjects
- reading books that expand your perspective
- engaging in thoughtful discussions
- solving puzzles or problems that interest you
- exploring new ideas through various media

Mental Decluttering

Just as physical clutter can create stress, mental clutter—unprocessed experiences, unfinished tasks, and unfocused thinking—can overwhelm your mind. Practice mental decluttering through:

- writing down tasks and ideas rather than trying to remember everything
- completing or consciously releasing unfinished projects
- making decisions you have been postponing
- creating clear mental categories rather than jumbling everything together
- regular periods of quiet to allow your mind to process and integrate

Social Self-Care

Quality Over Quantity

Social self-care is not about having the most friends or being constantly surrounded by people. It is about cultivating relationships that nourish rather than drain you. A few deep, authentic connections generally contribute more to well-being than many superficial ones.

Assess your relationships honestly. Which ones leave you feeling energised and supported? Which ones leave you feeling depleted or diminished? Invest more in the former while creating appropriate boundaries with the latter.

Communication and Boundaries

Healthy relationships require clear communication and respectful boundaries. Practice expressing your needs, preferences, and limits clearly while also remaining open to others' perspectives.

Remember that boundaries are not walls—they are guidelines that help you engage in relationships in ways that honour both yourself and others. Setting boundaries might involve specifying:

- how much time you can realistically give
- topics you are comfortable discussing
- types of support you can and cannot provide
- what behaviours you will and will not accept

Community and Belonging

We all need a sense of belonging—of being part of something larger than ourselves. This might come through family, friendship circles, spiritual communities, hobby groups, or professional networks.

If you feel a lack of community, consider joining groups that align with your values and interests. Start with small, manageable interactions and gradually build genuine, supportive connections.

Solitude and Social Balance

While connection is essential, so is solitude. Many people—especially those with more introverted tendencies—need regular time alone to recharge and reconnect with themselves.

Honour your need for solitude without judgment. Schedule regular periods of alone time for reflection, rest, or engaging in solo activities that bring you joy. This is not selfish—it is necessary for maintaining your emotional and mental wellbeing.

Spiritual Self-Care

Connection to Something Larger

Spiritual self-care involves connecting with something beyond your individual self—whether you conceptualise this as God, nature, the universe, humanity, or simply a greater purpose. This connection provides perspective and meaning that sustains you through life's challenges.

This does not necessarily mean religious practice (though it can). It means cultivating awareness of your place in the larger whole and developing a sense of reverence for life itself.

Meaning and Purpose

Humans naturally seek meaning. When we feel our lives have purpose—that we are contributing something valuable—we experience greater resilience and fulfilment. Your purpose might be expressed through your work, relationships, creative pursuits, community involvement, or simply how you approach daily life.
We will explore this subject in much greater depth in a later chapter called 'Discover and Live Your Life as the Real You'. For now, simply notice what stirs your heart and makes you feel most alive—these are clues pointing toward your deeper purpose.

Practices That Nurture Your Spirit

Regular spiritual practices help you maintain a connection with your deeper self and the larger whole. These might include:

- meditation or contemplative prayer
- time in nature
- creative expression
- sacred reading or study
- ritual or ceremony
- service to others
- gratitude practices

Experiment to find practices that resonate with you and incorporate them into your daily life.

Nature Connection

Many people find that time in natural settings restores their perspective and reconnects them with something larger than themselves. Whether it is a hike in the mountains, gardening, watching a sunset, or simply sitting under a tree, regular contact with nature can be deeply nourishing for your spirit.

Creating Your Personal Self-Care Practice

Assessing Your Needs

Self-Assessment

To create an effective self-care practice, first understand your current situation. For each dimension of self-care we have explored, ask yourself:

- How am I doing in this area on a scale of 1-10?
- What is working well?
- What is missing or needs attention?
- What small improvement would make the biggest difference?

Be honest but not judgmental in your assessment. The goal is clarity, not criticism.

Warning Signs of Self-Neglect

Learn to recognise your personal warning signs that self-care needs attention:

- Physical signs might include fatigue, frequent illness, tension, or disrupted sleep.
- Emotional signs might include irritability, numbness, or mood swings.
- Mental signs might include difficulty concentrating, negative thought patterns, or forgetfulness.
- Social signs might include withdrawal, conflict, or people-pleasing.
- Spiritual signs might include loss of purpose, disconnection, or cynicism.

The earlier you notice these signals, the easier it is to address them before they escalate.

Understanding Your Unique Requirements

Your self-care needs will vary based on your:

- constitutional type (dosha)
- current life stage and circumstances
- personal history and sensitivity patterns
- season and environment
- energy levels and health status

What works for someone else may not work for you. And what works for you today may not work tomorrow. Effective self-care requires ongoing attunement to your changing needs.

Designing Your Practice

Start Small and Build

Don't try to overhaul your entire life at once. Begin with one or two small practices that address your most pressing needs. For example:

- a 5-minute morning meditation
- a midday walk outside
- a technology-free evening hour
- a weekly bath ritual

Once these become habitual, gradually add additional practices. Small, consistent actions create more lasting change than grand gestures that quickly fade.

Integration Into Daily Life

The most sustainable self-care is not something extra you add to your to-do list—it is woven into the fabric of your daily life. Look for ways to infuse self-care into existing routines:

- Turn your morning shower into a mindfulness practice.
- Use your commute to practice breathing exercises or listen to uplifting audio.
- Transform meal preparation into a sensory experience.
- Make transitions between activities opportunities for brief check-ins.

Seasonal and Cyclical Approaches

Just as nature moves through seasons, your self-care needs shift in cycles. You might need more rest in winter, more social connection in summer, more structure in autumn, and more gentle movement in spring.

Women may also notice their needs shifting with hormonal cycles throughout the month. Track these patterns and adjust your self-care accordingly, honouring your body's natural rhythms rather than expecting consistent energy and needs.

Overcoming Obstacles

Addressing the 'Selfish' Myth

Many people, especially women, have been conditioned to believe that prioritising their own needs is selfish. Remember that caring for yourself makes you better able to care for others. It is like the aeroplane oxygen mask instructions—secure your own before helping others.

Self-care is not selfish; self-neglect is ultimately more damaging to oneself and others. When you are depleted, everyone around you experiences a diminished version of you.

Managing Time Constraints

'I don't have time for self-care' usually means 'I haven't prioritised self-care.' Look honestly at how you spend your time and what adjustments you could make:

- Reduce social media and screen time.
- Combine self-care with existing activities (like walking or meetings).
- Delegate or eliminate non-essential tasks.
- Say no to additional commitments.
- Wake up 15 minutes earlier for morning practices.

Remember that effective self-care often saves time in the long run by preventing burnout and illness.

Handling Resistance from Others

When you start prioritising your wellbeing, some people may resist these changes. They might be used to you being constantly available or may feel threatened by your new boundaries.

Communicate your needs clearly and compassionately.

Reassure others that taking care of yourself will ultimately benefit your relationships. Be prepared to consistently and respectfully reinforce boundaries.

Working With Limited Resources

Self-care does not have to be expensive or time-consuming. Many powerful practices are completely free:

- deep breathing
- walking outside
- journalling
- mindful awareness
- drinking water
- getting adequate sleep
- connecting with supportive friends

Focus on the essentials first. As your energy and resources grow through basic self-care, you will have more capacity for additional practices.

The Ripple Effects

When you genuinely love and care for yourself, the effects ripple outward in all directions. Your relationships improve because you are now full, rather than depleted. Your work becomes more effective because your best self is working on your tasks. Your health improves because you are addressing problems before they escalate. Your spiritual life deepens because you have the capacity for presence and contemplation.

This is not just ancient wisdom—it is a practical reality. The Law of Correspondence reminds us that our outer reality mirrors our inner landscape. When we cultivate love, respect, and care within ourselves, we naturally create more loving, respectful, and caring experiences outside.

Think of self-care not as a luxury or an indulgence, but as the foundation for everything else you hope to create and experience. By returning to who you truly are—a being worthy of love and care—you align with the Universal Laws and ancient wisdom that have guided human flourishing for millennia.

Your journey of rebecoming is a sacred one. Honour it by treating yourself with the love and care you deserve. Start today, start small, but start. Your whole life is waiting to transform.

The Healing Power of Self-Care

This is why self-care is not selfish—it is essential medicine. When you prioritise your well-being, you are not just improving your quality of life; you are literally supporting your body's ability to heal and thrive.

Emotional Self-Care helps release stored trauma and stress:

- processing emotions instead of suppressing them
- setting healthy boundaries
- practising forgiveness (of yourself and others)
- seeking support when you need it

Physical Self-Care supports your body's natural healing:

- nourishing yourself with healthy food
- moving your body regularly
- getting adequate rest and sleep
- creating environments that feel safe and peaceful

Mental Self-Care calms your nervous system:

- practising mindfulness and meditation
- engaging in activities that bring you joy
- limiting exposure to stress and negativity
- cultivating thoughts that support your well-being

Spiritual Self-Care connects you to something greater:

- spending time in nature
- engaging in practices that feel meaningful
- connecting with your inner wisdom
- cultivating gratitude and wonder

When you commit to genuine self-care and begin releasing your emotional baggage, something beautiful happens. Your nervous system starts to regulate. Your sleep improves. Your digestion settles. Your energy increases. You get sick less often, and when you do, you recover faster.

But the benefits go beyond the physical. You become more present with your loved ones. You make better decisions. You handle stress with more grace. You find more joy in simple pleasures. Your entire life begins to shift when your body feels safe and supported.

Instead of seeing your body as something that betrays you with illness or fatigue, begin to see it as your wise ally. Those aches, pains, and symptoms? They are often your body's way of saying, 'Please pay attention. Something needs care here.'

Listen to these messages with compassion. Your body has been working so hard to keep you going, often without the support it needs. When you begin to care for yourself with the same tenderness you would show a beloved friend, your body responds with gratitude and healing.

BUILD A HEALTHY RELATIONSHIP WITH MONEY

Ancient Wisdom & Universal Laws:

- *The Buddha's Middle Way and the Greek concept of eudaimonia reveal a profound truth: genuine prosperity comes not from grasping after wealth or denying it entirely, but from cultivating inner balance and living virtuously.*

- *Buddhism teaches freedom from attachment to material things, while eudaimonia points to human flourishing through purposeful living.*

- *The Law of Compensation aligns with this wisdom—true abundance flows naturally when you create genuine value while maintaining inner equilibrium. This ancient understanding illuminates the path of rebecoming: when you shift from acquiring to cultivating, financial serenity becomes a tool for living your highest purpose rather than the purpose itself.*

Imagine for a moment that money is a person in your life. How do you get on with money? Do you get on well? What do you think about money? How do you feel about money? How does money treat you?

These questions are not as odd as they might appear because, in a way, money is like a person. Money is something that you have a relationship with. You need it as much as you need the important people in your life. You have to deal with it daily, and, depending on how you interact with it, you get different reactions and results.

Just as we explored in previous chapters how emotional baggage from past events and relationships can weigh us down, we also carry similar baggage related to money. And just as healing those wounds allows us to move on in life, healing our money wounds opens the door to financial serenity—a state where money becomes a supportive tool rather than a source of stress.

Understanding Your Money Story

The Emotional Baggage of Money

Does any of this sound familiar?

- Are you drowning in debt, unsure how you will ever climb out?
- Do you struggle with a low income that never seems to cover all your expenses?
- Do you constantly feel like you are one step behind in your finances, always playing catch-up?
- Does thinking about money fill you with stress and anxiety?

If you answered yes to any of these questions, you are not alone. These financial challenges often stem from something deeper than just numbers in a bank account—they are rooted in the emotional baggage we carry about money.

Like the protective patterns we developed in response to past hurts, our relationship with money carries its own protection system. This baggage comprises all the painful experiences, hurtful words, and tough times we have had related to money. It is the anxiety you feel when checking your bank account, the shame when making a purchase, the fear of never having enough.

Your Money Protection System

When you have been hurt financially in the past—perhaps you grew up with scarcity, experienced a significant loss, or were taught that wanting money is selfish—your protection system kicks in. Just like the Bear and Wolf we discussed earlier, this financial protection system is trying to shield you from future pain.
It might make you:

- avoid looking at your finances (the ostrich approach)
- overspend to compensate for feelings of lack (filling an emotional void)
- cling too tightly to every penny out of fear (the scarcity grip)
- self-sabotage when financial success comes near (the unworthiness block)

These protective behaviours made sense at the time they developed, but now they might be keeping you from the financial peace you deserve.

Uncovering Your Money Mindset

Before you can transform your financial situation, you need to understand your money story—the narrative about your relationship with money that has been shaped by your experiences, family, and culture.

Take some time to reflect deeply. Writing down your answers can help bring subconscious patterns to light. Ask yourself:

About your past:

- What is your earliest memory about money?
- How was money discussed in your home growing up?
- What messages did you receive about wealth and poverty?
- Were there any significant financial traumas in your family history?

About your beliefs:

- What fears do you have about money?
- Do you feel worthy of financial abundance?
- What do you believe you would have to sacrifice to have more money?
- What does 'financial success' mean to you?

About your patterns:

- How do you feel when you pay bills? Make purchases? Save money?
- What emotions come up when you think about your financial future?
- Do you tend to overspend or underspend? Why?
- What financial behaviours do you engage in when stressed?

Do this reflection exercise over several days. Like peeling an onion, it may take time for deeper beliefs to surface. You will likely discover that many of your thoughts about money were inherited—programmed into you before you could form your own opinions.

From Survival to Serenity

Calming the Financial Storm

Just as we learned to calm our emotional storms in previous chapters, we need to soothe our financial anxiety before we can make lasting changes. When you are in financial survival mode, your brain can not access its full problem-solving capacity.

Immediate calming practices:

- Take three deep breaths before any financial task
- Place your hand on your heart and remind yourself: 'My net worth does not determine my worth'
- Create a calming ritual around money tasks (light a candle, play soothing music)

Practical first steps:

- Gather all your financial information without judgment—just observe
- Create a simple snapshot of where you are: income, expenses, debts, assets
- Set up separate accounts for different purposes (spending, saving, goals)
- Identify one small, achievable financial goal to build confidence

Self-compassion practices:

- Talk to yourself about money mistakes as you would to a dear friend
- Remember that everyone makes financial missteps—it is how we learn
- Celebrate small wins, like looking at your bank balance or paying a bill on time

Moving from Scarcity to Sufficiency

The scarcity mindset—the deep belief that there is never enough—often drives our financial stress. This mindset keeps us trapped in a cycle of fear and grasping, preventing us from making clear financial decisions or enjoying what we have.

The path from scarcity to sufficiency is not about having more money; it is about shifting your relationship with what you have. This is where ancient wisdom offers guidance. The concept of 'enough' is not about settling for less—it is about recognising abundance in its many forms.

Practice noticing abundance:

- Keep a gratitude journal specifically for financial blessings, however small

- Notice the wealth in your life beyond money: relationships, skills, experiences
- Challenge scarcity thoughts with evidence of provision in your past
- Share or give something small regularly to reinforce the flow of abundance

The Middle Way with Money

The Buddhist Middle Way teaches us to avoid extremes—neither grasping desperately nor rejecting entirely. Applied to money, this means finding a balance between responsible planning and trusting in life's flow.

This middle way looks like:

- Planning without obsessing: Create budgets as guides, not rigid rules.
- Saving without hoarding: Build security while staying generous.
- Spending without guilt: Enjoy the benefits of money while staying conscious.
- Working without sacrificing your well-being: Earn in alignment with your values.
- Receiving without shame: Accept financial help or windfalls gracefully.

The middle way recognises that money is energy—meant to flow, not stagnate. When we grip too tightly, we block the flow. When we are too loose, we lose stability. The art is finding your unique balance point.

Recognising Emotional Triggers

Now that you have calmed the storm and begun shifting from scarcity, you can start the deeper healing work. Begin by becoming a detective of your own emotional responses to money.

When you notice a strong emotional reaction, pause and explore:

- What specific situation triggered this feeling?
- Where do you feel it in your body?
- What story is your mind telling you about this situation?
- What fear is underneath this reaction?
- What would love do in this situation?

For example, if checking your bank balance triggers anxiety, the story might be 'I'm irresponsible with money,' the fear might be 'I'll end up homeless.' Love might say, 'I'm learning and growing in my financial awareness.'

Challenging Limiting Beliefs

Once you have identified your emotional patterns and their underlying beliefs, you can begin questioning and transforming them. Remember, these beliefs are like outdated software in your protection system—they need to be updated.

For each limiting belief you discover, ask:

- Is this belief absolutely true?
- How did I come to believe this?
- How has this belief protected me in the past?
- What has this belief cost me?
- What would I rather believe instead?
- What evidence supports this new belief?

Common money beliefs to examine:

- Seek to shift from 'Money is the root of all evil' to 'Money is a neutral tool that amplifies who I am'
- Seek to shift from 'Rich people are greedy' to 'Wealth allows me to contribute more to others'
- Seek to shift from 'I'm bad with money' to 'I'm learning to manage money with increasing skill'
- Seek to shift from 'There's never enough' to 'I have enough for today and am building for tomorrow'

Practical Healing Techniques

The Money Dialogue

Set aside time for a written dialogue with money. Write as yourself, then write money's response. This might feel silly at first, but it can reveal surprising insights:

- You: 'Why do you always seem to disappear?'
- Money: 'You push me away because you don't feel worthy of keeping me.'
- You: 'How can we work better together?'
- Money: 'Treat me with respect—track me, appreciate me, use me consciously.'

Financial Forgiveness Practice

Just as we forgive people who have hurt us, it helps to forgive our financial past:

- forgive yourself for past money mistakes
- forgive family members whose money behaviours affected you
- forgive the circumstances that led to financial hardship
- forgive the system that may have disadvantaged you

Write a forgiveness letter to yourself about your financial past. Include compassion for the person you were, doing the best you could with what you knew.

Rewriting Your Money Story

Create a new narrative about your relationship with money. Write it in the present tense, as if it is already true: 'I have a peaceful, balanced relationship with money. I manage it with wisdom and use it to support my values. Money flows to me as I create value for others. I save with joy and spend with consciousness. I am worthy of financial abundance and use it to benefit myself and others.'

Using Money as a Tool for Values

The deepest healing comes when we align our financial life with our true values. Money then becomes not the goal, but the tool that helps us live our purpose.
Identify your core values, then explore:

- How can money support these values?
- What financial choices would honour these values?
- How would someone who holds these values handle money?
- What would financial success look like through the lens of these values?

For example, if freedom is a core value, financial success might mean having enough saved to take unpaid time off, rather than earning the highest possible salary at a restrictive job.

Living in Financial Serenity

What a Healthy Money Relationship Looks Like

When you have healed your money wounds and aligned your finances with your values, you will notice distinct changes:

Inner changes:

- checking your accounts feels neutral or even pleasant
- financial decisions come from clarity rather than fear
- you trust yourself to handle money challenges
- unexpected expenses do not trigger panic
- you feel grateful for what you have while working toward goals

Outer changes:

- you have enough money
- your financial life has order without rigidity
- you make conscious spending choices without guilt
- you save naturally as an act of self-care
- you can be generous without depleting yourself
- you discuss money openly and without shame

Maintaining Balance

Financial serenity is not a destination you reach once—it is an ongoing practice. Here is how to maintain your healthy money relationship:

Daily practices:

- Brief morning gratitude for yesterday's financial blessings
- Conscious breathing before any money transaction
- Evening acknowledgement of the day's financial choices

Weekly practices:

- Regular money date with yourself (or partner) to review and plan
- Celebrating financial wins, however small
- Adjusting your budget with compassion, not criticism

Monthly practices:

- Reviewing your financial progress without

judgment
- Checking if your spending is aligned with your values
- Setting intentions for the coming month

For couples, creating financial serenity in a partnership requires special attention:

- Share your money stories with each other compassionately
- Create shared financial goals while respecting individual needs
- Divide money tasks according to each person's strengths
- Maintain some financial autonomy alongside shared resources
- Celebrate financial victories together
- Face financial challenges as a team, not adversaries

Remember the 'yours, mine, and ours' approach—maintaining some separate accounts alongside shared ones can reduce money conflicts and preserve healthy autonomy.

The Freedom of Financial Peace

When you have built a healthy relationship with money, you experience a freedom that transcends your bank balance. This freedom includes:

- making choices from abundance rather than fear
- pursuing work that aligns with your purpose
- being generous with others and yourself
- planning for the future while enjoying the present
- seeing money as one form of wealth among many
- trusting in your ability to create and manage resources

This does not mean you will never face financial challenges. But when you do, you will meet them from a place of inner stability rather than panic. You will have the tools to navigate difficulties without losing your centre.

Financial serenity is about having a peaceful and calm relationship with money, regardless of how much you have. It is about knowing your worth is not measured by how much money you have, while also seeing money as a useful tool for creating the life you want.

As you continue this journey, remember that healing your

relationship with money is part of your larger journey of rebecoming. Each step toward financial serenity is a step toward living as the real you—someone who relates to all of life, including money, from a place of love rather than fear.

The path may not always be smooth, but with patience, self-compassion, and consistent practice, you can transform your relationship with money from a source of stress to a supportive partnership. And in doing so, you free yourself to focus on what truly matters—living a life aligned with your deepest values and highest purpose.

RAISE YOUR LIFE FORCE

Ancient Wisdom & Universal Laws:

- *What ancient traditions call qi, prana, or life force, the Law of Vibration reveals as your energetic frequency—constantly influenced by your thoughts, environment, and practices. Through this universal principle, everything from your cells to your consciousness exists in a state of perpetual motion and resonance.*
- *Yogic teachings state that vitality comes from aligning your personal energy with nature's rhythms and balancing receptive yin with active yang energies. This ancient understanding illuminates the path of rebecoming: as you consciously cultivate your life force, you raise your vibrational frequency and access a wellspring of vitality that transforms not just your health, but your entire experience of being alive.*

Picture this: You wake up feeling energised. Your mind is clear, your body feels strong, and you are genuinely excited about the day ahead. This is not just about having more energy - it is about feeling fully alive, vibrant, and ready to embrace whatever life brings your way. This is what it feels like when your life force is strong.

What exactly is life force? Ancient traditions across the world recognise it by different names - ojas in Ayurveda, chi in Chinese medicine, prana in yoga. Think of it as your vital energy, the fundamental power that animates your body, mind, and spirit. It is not just the energy that keeps you physically active; it is the sparkle in your eyes, the warmth in your smile, the resilience in your spirit, and the clarity in your mind.

In our modern world, we are facing a life force crisis. We are running on artificial energy - caffeine kicks, sugar highs, and adrenaline rushes. We push ourselves through long days, fighting our natural rhythms and ignoring our body's signals. We are constantly connected to devices but disconnected from our own vital energy. The result? Many of us are walking around with depleted life force, wondering why we feel so exhausted despite getting enough sleep, why we catch every cold going around, or why we have lost our zest for life.

How can you tell if your life force is strong or depleted? Your body and mind give you clear signals:

Signs of Strong Life Force:

- Natural energy that lasts throughout the day
- Resilient immune system
- Quick recovery from stress or illness
- Stable mood and emotional balance
- Mental clarity and sharp focus
- Healthy appetite and digestion
- Restful sleep and easy awakening
- Strong sense of purpose and enthusiasm
- Natural ability to handle life's challenges
- Magnetic personality that draws others to you

Signs of Depleted Life Force:

- Chronic fatigue or reliance on stimulants
- Frequent illness or slow healing
- Difficulty bouncing back from setbacks
- Mood swings or emotional fragility
- Brain fog and poor concentration
- Irregular appetite or digestive issues
- Disturbed sleep patterns
- Lack of motivation or purpose
- Feeling overwhelmed by small challenges
- Social withdrawal or relationship struggles

The good news is that your life force is not fixed. Just as a depleted battery can be recharged, your vital energy can be restored and strengthened. In fact, working with your life force is one of the most powerful ways to transform your health, happiness, and overall quality of life.

In this chapter, we will explore how to build and protect your life force using both ancient wisdom and modern understanding. You will learn practical techniques to increase your vital energy, protect it from common drains, and maintain it at optimal levels. Whether you are feeling completely depleted or just wanting to boost your natural vitality, you will find tools and practices that can help.

Remember, raising your life force is not just about having more energy; it is about enhancing your entire life experience. When your life force is strong, you are more resilient to stress, more resistant to illness, more creative in your thinking, and more magnetic in your presence. You have more to give to others because your own cup is full.

Across time and cultures, people have recognised a vital energy that goes beyond just physical strength or mental alertness.

This fundamental life energy has been understood and described in fascinating ways by different traditions.

In Ayurveda, ojas refers to the pure essence of life that gives you vigour, immunity, and radiance. Think of ojas as the honey of your body's biochemistry. Just as bees transform flower nectar into rich, golden honey, your body transforms food, experiences, and practices into this subtle yet powerful essence. When your ojas is strong, you literally glow with health and vitality.

Chinese medicine refers to 'chi' or 'qi', the vital force that flows through specific pathways in the body, much like rivers of energy. When chi flows freely, you experience health and vitality. When it is blocked or depleted, illness and fatigue follow. This is why practices like acupuncture and Qi Gong focus on keeping these energy channels clear and flowing.

Yoga tradition talks about 'prana' - the life force that rides on your breath and animates your entire being. Every breath you take can either enhance or diminish your prana. This is why yogic practices place so much emphasis on conscious breathing, as it is a direct way to influence your life force.

The Science of Vitality

While these ancient concepts might sound mystical, modern science is beginning to understand the biological basis of life force. Here is what research tells us:

- Your body's cells contain tiny powerhouses called mitochondria that generate energy. The more efficiently these work, the more vitality you experience.
- Your autonomic nervous system affects everything from your heart rate to your digestion. When it is balanced, you feel energised yet calm.
- Your endocrine system produces hormones that influence your energy, mood, and resilience. Balanced hormones mean balanced vitality.
- A strong life force is reflected in a robust immune system that efficiently protects and repairs your body.

Your life force is not just about physical health - it influences every aspect of your experience:

Life Areas	Strong Life Force	Depleted Life Force
Mental Clarity	Sharp Focus & Clear Thinking	Brain Fog & Scattered Thoughts
Emotional Balance	Emotional Resilience & Stable Mood	Emotional Fragility & Mood Swings
Physical Vitality	Natural Energy & Quick Recovery	Fatigue & Slow Healing
Spiritual Connection	Sense Of Purpose & Meaning	Feeling Lost or Disconnected
Relationships	Magnetic Presence & Healthy Boundaries	Neediness or Withdrawal
Creativity	Flowing Inspiration & Expression	Creative Blocks & Stagnation
Success and Achievement	Natural Motivation & Persistence	Procrastination & Giving Up Easily

Think of your life force as electricity in your home. When the power is strong and steady, everything works well: the lights are bright, appliances run efficiently, and life flows comfortably. But when the power fluctuates or dims, everything is affected. Some things stop working entirely, while others function below their capacity.

The life force is not static—various factors constantly influence it. There are numerous ways to build and strengthen your life force. These positive influences include:

- restful sleep
- nourishing food
- time in nature
- loving relationships
- meaningful work
- creative expression
- physical movement
- spiritual practices

The key is understanding that you are not a passive recipient of life force—you are actively involved in either building or depleting it through your daily choices and habits. Each decision you make throughout the day either feeds your energy or drains it. By becoming more conscious of these choices, you can take control of your vitality and create a life that feels energised rather than exhausted.

Managing Your Life Force

Your life force is as unique as your fingerprint. Some people naturally radiate high energy, while others maintain a quieter, steadier vitality. The key is not matching someone else's pattern, but understanding and optimising your own natural rhythm.

Discover Your Personal Energy Pattern

Start by observing yourself for a week. Notice when your energy naturally peaks and dips throughout the day. Are you a morning person who wakes up ready to tackle the world? Or do you find your creative flow in the evening hours? Pay attention to:

- what times of day you feel most alert and focused
- which activities leave you feeling energised versus drained
- how different foods affect your energy levels
- how much sleep your body truly needs to feel refreshed
- which people in your life boost your energy and which deplete it

This self-awareness becomes the foundation for creating a life that works in harmony with your natural rhythms, rather than against them.

Protect Your Energy Like a Precious Resource

Think of your life force as your daily energy allowance, which requires careful management. Just as you protect your financial savings, you need to protect your energy from unnecessary drains. Many of us unknowingly leak energy through unconscious habits, difficult relationships, or environments that do not support our well-being.

This protection starts with creating clear boundaries in five key areas:

- Time boundaries: Schedule your day to align with your natural energy peaks. If you are sharpest in the morning, tackle your most demanding tasks then. Create specific periods for work, rest, and recharging that align with your personal rhythm.
- Relationship boundaries: Notice who consistently drains your energy and limit your exposure to them when possible. For those relationships you cannot change (like certain family or work connections), develop strategies to protect yourself during interactions.
- Digital boundaries: Your attention is a form of energy. Create a structure around technology use that works for your specific needs – perhaps no screens before breakfast or after 9 PM, or social media only at designated times.
- Physical boundaries: Honour your body's unique needs for rest, movement, and nourishment. The generic advice to 'exercise daily' might need adjusting – perhaps you thrive with gentle morning yoga rather than intense evening workouts.
- Emotional boundaries: Choose when and how deeply to engage with others' energy based on your current capacity. Some days you may have more to give than others.

Listen to Your Body's Signals

Your body has its own way of telling you when your energy needs protection. Pay attention to your personal warning signs, which might include:

- a particular type of headache that only comes when you are overstimulated
- a specific feeling of heaviness in your chest when you are taking on too much
- disrupted sleep patterns unique to when you are energy-depleted
- changes in your appetite or digestion
- your own version of emotional overwhelm (irritability, tearfulness, numbness)

These are not just random symptoms – they are your body's sophisticated feedback system letting you know it is time to implement 'energy hygiene practices' tailored to your needs.

Create Your Personal Energy Toolkit

Experiment with different practices to discover which ones most effectively replenish your specific energy pattern:

- For mental overload: You might find that a 10-minute meditation works wonders, or perhaps journaling helps you more effectively process and release thoughts.
- For physical stagnation: Discover what type of movement recharges rather than depletes you. This could be a brisk walk, gentle stretching, dance, or even gardening.
- For emotional heaviness: Perhaps time in nature resets your emotional energy, or a meaningful conversation with a specific friend helps you process feelings.
- For spiritual disconnection: Identify which practices help you reconnect with your deeper self – it might be prayer, time in silence, creative expression, or community connection.

Build your personal toolkit with 5-7 reliable practices that you know will restore your energy when it is depleted.

Create Your Energy Shield for Challenging Situations

We all face energy-draining situations that we cannot avoid. Develop your personalised 'energy shield' technique for these times:

- Perhaps visualising a protective bubble around yourself works for you.
- Or maybe having a specific phrase you repeat internally helps maintain your boundaries.
- Some find that wearing a particular item (such as a special piece of jewellery) serves as a physical reminder to maintain energy boundaries.

Practice your shield technique regularly so it becomes second nature when you need it most.

DEVELOP HARMONY BETWEEN YOUR MASCULINE AND FEMININE NATURE

Ancient Wisdom & Universal Laws:

- *The Taoist symbol of yin-yang and the Tantric union of Shiva-Shakti reveal what the Law of Gender confirms: creation emerges from the sacred dance between masculine and feminine energies within each being.*

- *The Law of Polarity teaches that these complementary forces—structure and flow, action and receptivity, logic and intuition—exist not in opposition but in dynamic harmony. This ancient understanding illuminates the path of rebecoming. As you heal and balance these primal energies within yourself, you access a wholeness that transforms not just your relationships, but your creative potential and purpose in the world.*

As you have been working through the process of releasing your emotional baggage, you have already begun the journey toward balancing these fundamental energies. In this chapter, we will explore how to develop true harmony between your masculine and feminine nature, allowing you to access your full potential and authentic power.

The Natural Emergence of Harmony

As you release your emotional baggage, something remarkable happens—those wounded expressions of masculine and feminine energy naturally begin to fade. It is like clearing clouds from the sky; what emerges is the natural, balanced state of these energies that was there all along.

When you heal the pain of rejection, that wounded feminine energy of neediness and victimhood starts to dissolve. When you process old anger and fear, that wounded masculine drive for control and dominance begins to soften. The wounded expressions are not actually part of your true nature—they are protective responses to pain and trauma.

This is why the work you did in the previous chapter on emotional baggage is so crucial. By addressing those deeper wounds, you are not just healing past hurts—you are also freeing your natural energies to express themselves in healthy ways. You do not need to specifically focus on 'fixing' wounded masculine or feminine traits. Instead, as you release the emotional baggage that created them, these distorted expressions naturally return to their balanced state.

It is like cleaning a window—you don't need to create the sunlight; you just need to remove what blocks it. Similarly, you do not need to create healthy masculine and feminine energies—they are already within you. You just need to clear away the emotional debris that is preventing them from shining through.

This healing process works on two important levels. First, as we have discussed, healing emotional wounds naturally 'unwounds' the distorted expressions of masculine and feminine energies. When you heal the traumas that caused you to adopt these protective patterns, you naturally return to a more balanced state without having to focus directly on the masculine-feminine dynamic itself.

Second, as you questioned social and cultural expectations in the 'Break Free from Being Controlled' chapter, you have already begun to recognise how society has shaped your understanding of masculine and feminine energies. Our culture often dictates rigid roles—men should be strong and unemotional (overly masculine), while women should be accommodating and nurturing (overly feminine). By questioning these external and extreme definitions, you create space to discover the truth: that all humans naturally possess both energies, regardless of gender.

As you continue to challenge these artificial limitations, you will find it easier to embrace all aspects of yourself. The masculine strength and feminine compassion within you are not in competition—they are complementary parts of your whole self that have always belonged together. Recognising this integration within yourself is a powerful step toward authentic living.

The Dance of Energies

Think of balancing your energies like a dance. Sometimes you lead (masculine), sometimes you follow (feminine). Sometimes you move with structured precision (masculine), sometimes with flowing spontaneity (feminine). The beauty is not in holding perfectly still in the middle—it is in moving gracefully between these different qualities as each moment requires.

This integration dance is dynamic and ever-changing. There is no fixed formula or perfect ratio of masculine to feminine energy that works for everyone or in every situation. Instead, true harmony comes from developing the flexibility to move between these energies with awareness and intention. Imagine a skilled dancer who knows exactly when to step forward with confidence and when to yield with grace, when to provide structure and when to flow with creativity. This dancer does not get stuck in one mode or position but responds organically to the music, their partner, and the moment.

Similarly, when your masculine and feminine energies are in harmony, you will find yourself naturally knowing when to be strong and when to be soft, when to push forward and when to pause, when to speak and when to listen. This is not about following rules or forcing yourself into particular ways of being—it is about allowing your natural wisdom to guide you.

As you heal your emotional baggage, this dance becomes more natural. The wounded patterns that once caused you to overcompensate with rigid control or collapse into dependency begin to dissolve, making way for the authentic expression of your whole self.

Recognition Tools

How do you know when you are in balance versus when you have slipped into wounded expressions? Your body and emotions provide valuable feedback if you learn to recognise the signs.

Signs of Natural Balance

You will know you are finding your natural balance when:

- you can be strong without being aggressive
- you can be nurturing without losing yourself
- you feel comfortable both leading and following
- you can express emotions without being overwhelmed by them
- you can take action without being controlling
- you can receive help without feeling weak
- you trust both your logic and your intuition
- you feel a sense of internal harmony rather than inner conflict
- your decisions feel aligned with both your head and your heart
- you can adapt your approach based on what each

situation needs

Signs of Imbalance

Conversely, you might notice you have slipped into imbalance when:

- you feel a need to dominate or control situations (wounded masculine)
- you feel unable to make decisions without others' approval (wounded feminine)
- you are rigidly attached to plans and become frustrated when they change (wounded masculine)
- you consistently prioritise others' needs at the expense of your own (wounded feminine)
- you shut down emotionally during conflict (wounded masculine)
- you become overwhelmed by emotions and unable to think clearly (wounded feminine)
- you feel you must always be strong and never show vulnerability (wounded masculine)
- you feel powerless to set boundaries or say no (wounded feminine)

Practice checking in with yourself regularly. Notice which energy you are expressing and whether it feels natural or forced. Are you pushing to be 'strong' when you really need to be receptive? Are you being passive when you need to take action? These awareness moments help you adjust and stay balanced.

Situational Flexibility

While balance is the goal, different situations require varying proportions of masculine and feminine energy. The key is developing the flexibility to consciously draw on each energy as needed.

Leadership roles may require more of your masculine qualities—such as decisiveness, strategic thinking, and clear boundaries. Creative projects might benefit from more feminine energy—intuition, receptivity to inspiration, and fluid thinking. Close relationships often require a beautiful dance between both energies—the masculine ability to hold space and the feminine capacity for deep connection.

Here are some examples of when you might intentionally call on more of one energy:

Situations calling for more masculine energy:

- setting boundaries with someone who consistently oversteps
- launching a new business or project
- making important financial decisions
- advocating for yourself or others
- executing a plan with clear steps and timelines

Situations calling for more feminine energy:

- listening deeply to a friend in need
- brainstorming creative solutions to a problem
- building meaningful connections in your community
- tuning into your intuition when something feels off
- allowing yourself to receive support or guidance

The goal is not to suppress either energy but to develop the wisdom to know which is needed in any given moment, and the flexibility to access it naturally. This situational flexibility is a hallmark of true integration.

Balance in Relationships

Your ability to dance between masculine and feminine energies directly affects the quality of your relationships. When you are in balance, you bring your whole self to your connections with others—both the strength and the softness, the structure and the flow.

In personal relationships, this balance allows for deeper intimacy and authenticity. You can be vulnerable without becoming dependent, and you can be strong without becoming domineering. You can give without depleting yourself, and receive without feeling inadequate.

In professional relationships, this balance enables you to lead with both clarity and compassion, to hold firm to your vision while remaining open to collaboration. You can set clear expectations while still being approachable, and you can listen to feedback without taking it personally.

Many relationship struggles stem from imbalances in these energies. Perhaps you have experienced a partnership where one person always made the decisions (overly masculine) while the other always accommodated (overly feminine). Or maybe you have been in work situations where rigid structure stifled creativity, or where a lack of boundaries led to chaos.

As you develop more balance within yourself, you will naturally create more balanced relationships. You will be drawn to people who can also dance between these energies, and you will find yourself less triggered by or attracted to wounded expressions in others.

Responding to Wounded Energies in Others

In our journey to heal and balance our own masculine and feminine energies, we inevitably encounter others who are operating from wounded aspects of these energies. Whether it is a partner displaying controlling behaviour, a colleague who manipulates through victimhood, or a family member who swings between domination and passive-aggression, these interactions can challenge our own balance and healing process.

There is a common misconception that we should respond to wounded masculine energy with strong masculine energy or counter wounded feminine traits with healthy feminine attributes. This overly simplistic approach often backfires, leading to power struggles or enabling unhealthy dynamics to persist.

The truth is far more nuanced. When faced with someone operating from wounded energy—whether masculine or feminine—the most effective response is not found in opposites but in balance.

Before exploring how to respond effectively, let us remind ourselves what these wounded expressions look like:

- *Wounded Masculine* often appears as domination, aggression, rigidity, emotional shutdown, excessive control, criticism, or abuse of power.
- *Wounded Feminine* typically shows itself as manipulation, excessive dependence, indirect communication, martyrdom, emotional volatility, passive-aggression, or boundary violations through 'helping' or 'nurturing.'

Both these wounded expressions stem from the same place: unmet needs, unhealed trauma, and defensive protection systems designed to prevent further pain.

When dealing with someone displaying wounded energies, the most powerful tool is a balanced approach. This means drawing consciously from both your healthy masculine and feminine qualities in response to the situation.

Responding to Wounded Masculine Energy

When facing someone who is displaying domination, control, or aggression, you will need:

- clear boundaries (healthy masculine) that establish what behaviour you will and will not accept
- grounded presence (healthy masculine) that does not match aggression but does not collapse either
- compassionate understanding (healthy feminine) of the fear or insecurity driving their behaviour
- emotional intelligence (healthy feminine) to navigate the interaction without escalating it

For example, when someone behaves aggressively towards you, rather than meeting fire with fire (wounded masculine) or placating them to keep the peace (wounded feminine), you might calmly state: 'I understand you are frustrated, but I need you to speak to me respectfully. I am happy to discuss this when we can both communicate more effectively.'

This response combines the boundary-setting of healthy masculine with the relational awareness of healthy feminine.

Responding to Wounded Feminine Energy

When dealing with passive-aggression, manipulation, or emotional volatility, your balanced response might include:

- direct communication (healthy masculine) that addresses issues straightforwardly
- consistent follow-through (healthy masculine) on the consequences you have established
- empathetic listening (healthy feminine) that acknowledges genuine emotions
- intuitive awareness (healthy feminine) of what is happening beneath the surface

For instance, if someone is using emotional manipulation, rather than shutting down (wounded masculine) or getting caught in their emotional web (wounded feminine), you might say: 'I can see you're upset, and I want to understand. At the same time, I would like us to address this issue directly rather than through hints or implications. Can we talk about what is really bothering you?'

While this balanced approach is powerful, it is equally

important to recognise when a situation or relationship is too damaging to engage with. No amount of balanced response can fix deeply entrenched patterns of abuse or control from others.

The bringing together of masculine and feminine qualities should include the feminine wisdom to recognise what is not healthy for you and the masculine strength to walk away when necessary. Self-protection is not selfish—it is an essential part of wholeness.

DISCOVER AND LIVE YOUR LIFE AS THE REAL YOU

Ancient Wisdom & Universal Laws:

- *The Buddhist concept of dharma and indigenous vision quests point to what the Hermetic Principle of Mentalism confirms: your unique purpose exists first as a seed within your consciousness before it manifests in the world.*

- *The Laws of Assumption, Attraction, and Action work in harmony—first by believing in the possibility of your path, then by aligning your energy with it, and finally by taking inspired steps to bridge your vision and reality. This ancient understanding illuminates the journey of rebecoming: as you discover and embrace your authentic purpose, you participate in the sacred act of creation that transforms not just your individual life, but adds to the greater harmony of existence.*

Think back for a moment. Is there a quiet voice inside you that whispers there is more to life than the roles you are playing? This chapter is your invitation to listen to that inner voice. It is about the journey of rediscovering yourself beneath all the layers of who you think you should be.

We are not talking about another set of self-improvement techniques or strategies to be 'better.' Instead, we will explore what it means to peel away the expectations, beliefs, and patterns that have covered up your true self. It is time to remember who you were before the world told you who to be—and to bring the real you into every aspect of your life.

The Journey to Authentic Living

Living authentically is not just a nice idea—it is an entirely different way of being in the world. Instead of following the well-worn path of expectations and 'shoulds,' it means aligning with your most profound truth and what we will call your soul. This is not some distant, mystical concept—it is that quiet, wise part of you that has always been there.

Think of it as the patient Owl we have been discussing throughout this book, perched within, watching everything with clear-eyed wisdom. Your soul is the wisdom within you, observing your journey with compassion and understanding, offering guidance you may have been too busy or overwhelmed to hear. Just as an owl sees clearly in the darkness, your soul sees past the confusion and noise of daily life to what truly matters for your authentic path.

It is essential to recognise that the life you have lived up to this point is not something to regret or view as wasted time. Rebecoming the real you is part of the human experience—we all need to walk through these earlier chapters of our lives to reach this point of awakening. Those roles you have played, the masks you have worn, even the times you have felt lost or inauthentic—they have all been necessary steps on your path. They have taught you valuable lessons and helped shape your understanding of who you really are.

Your Inner Landscape Transforms

This stage of life marks a profound shift in your inner forest. Where once the Wolf patrolled anxiously, always on guard against threats, and the Bear reacted instinctively to rescue you from pain, now it is time for the Owl to take its rightful place as the guide of your inner world. Your protective animals have served you well—they kept you safe when danger was real. But in this new chapter, they can finally rest more often, their hypervigilance no longer needed in the same way.

The gentle Deer of your emotional self, once hiding in the shadows, can now venture into sunlit clearings as they are healed of their wounds. These Deer represent your natural capacity for joy, connection, and peaceful presence—aspects of yourself that may have been sacrificed in the name of safety and survival. As you honour the wisdom of the Owl, these Deer can once again move freely, teaching you to follow what truly feels good and nourishing.

Your clever Raven—that part of your mind that never stops thinking—also transforms. Once it exhausted you with endless analysis and fearful stories. Now, you can direct that same mental energy toward your goals. The Raven's problem-solving skills, which used to keep you trapped in cycles of rumination and anxiety, become practical tools for creating the life you want. Its voice changes too—becoming quieter, more focused, and more helpful. No longer the chaotic force that dominated your thoughts, the Raven becomes a skilled partner in bringing your deepest aspirations to life.

The Clearing Process

Imagine coming home after a long journey to find your house filled with years of accumulated stuff that is not really yours.

Perhaps there are gifts you never wanted but felt obliged to keep, furniture chosen to impress others rather than bring you joy, or decorations that matched someone else's taste. Now, picture clearing all of that away to reveal the beautiful framework of the house—its authentic character and charm.

That is what the journey back to your real self feels like. It is about gently removing the layers of beliefs, behaviours, and patterns you have collected over the years that do not truly belong to you.

This is not always a comfortable process. You have probably spent years building up these layers—ways of thinking, acting, and being that helped you fit in, stay safe, or meet others' expectations. These patterns served you well at one time, your Wolf and Bear creating protective strategies that helped you navigate challenging situations. However, these same patterns may now be holding you back from living as your true self.

The good news is that beneath these accumulated layers lies something precious and unchanging—the real you, the wisdom of your Owl, waiting to be heard and followed as you step into this new phase of authentic living.

Understanding the Real You

Remember when you were a child before the world started telling you who to be? What lit you up with joy? What made you feel most alive, and what did you dream about before others told you what was practical? These are not just idle memories—they are clues to your authentic self.

Your job title, relationships, or achievements do not define the real you. It goes beyond the roles you play or the masks you wear. Instead, think of the real you as your unique Soul Signature—like a spiritual fingerprint that makes you distinctly you. Just as your physical DNA shapes your unique physical traits, your Soul Signature shapes your natural way of being in the world.

This signature is not something you need to create—it already exists within you, waiting to be recognised and expressed. It is present in how you naturally approach challenges, the energy you bring to a room, and the distinctive way you touch others' lives when you are being genuine.

Unveiling Your Soul Signature

Your Soul Signature has been with you since birth. Rather than creating something new, think of it like a beautiful statue already existing within a block of marble. Your job is not to build the statue—it is to carefully chip away everything that is not truly yours until your authentic form is revealed.

This unveiling process can be both exciting and challenging, often requiring you to let go of old identities and beliefs. As you peel away the layers of who you think you should be, who others want you to be, and who you have learned to be to fit in, you uncover something honest, natural, and uniquely your own.

Remember, your Soul Signature does not need fixing or improving—it is perfect exactly as it is. Our work is simply to recognise it, trust it, and let it shine through more fully in daily life. The world does not need another copy of someone else; it needs your authentic way of being. When you are truly yourself, you bring something to the world that no one else can offer.

Understanding the real you means exploring three core aspects that make up your Soul Signature:

- *Your Essence & Gifts*: The natural qualities and talents that flow effortlessly from you.
- *Your Struggles & Lessons*: The challenges and themes that appear in your life to help you grow.
- *Your Purpose & Path*: How your unique gifts and learned wisdom come together to create your distinctive contribution to the world.

As we explore these elements, you will gain a clearer picture of who you truly are and what you are here to contribute.

Your Core Essence & Natural Gifts

At your core, you have a natural way of being - your essence. Think about how you are when you are entirely yourself, perhaps with close friends or doing something you love. Are you quietly thoughtful? Energetically expressive? Gently nurturing? This natural temperament is not something you chose or created - it is simply who you are.

Your essence also reveals itself through your deepest values - the principles and ideals that naturally matter most to you, not what others have told you should matter. These might include values such as freedom, connection, or honesty. They become your inner compass, guiding your authentic decisions and actions.

Interestingly, even your protection systems—the ways you have learned to safeguard yourself from emotional pain—contain important clues about your true essence and gifts. These protective responses did not develop randomly; they formed around your natural strengths and abilities. What you use to protect yourself often reflects what comes most naturally to you.

For instance, if you recognise the Appease response in yourself - people-pleasing and prioritising others' needs - this points to natural gifts of empathy, service, and relationship-building. Your tendency to sense others' emotions and adapt to their needs, though perhaps overdeveloped as a protective strategy, stems from authentic talents for connection and nurturing.

Similarly, those with Fight responses often have natural gifts for leadership, clarity, and setting boundaries. Those with Flight responses typically possess genuine talents for achievement, efficiency, and creative problem-solving. And those who Appease often have natural gifts for contemplation, observation, and deep thinking.

Your essence expresses itself through these natural gifts - the abilities that flow so effortlessly from you that you might not even recognise them as special. These are not just skills you have learned; they are the innate talents that are part of your authentic makeup. These gifts generally fall into several categories:

<u>Core Character Strengths:</u>

- Being naturally stable and grounded
- Showing resilience and determination
- Expressing confidence and self-assurance
- Thinking logically and maintaining focus
- Being alert and perceptive
- Working accurately and methodically
- Demonstrating independence and self-reliance

<u>Heart & Interpersonal Qualities:</u>

- Showing natural compassion and empathy
- Being open-hearted and loving
- Expressing sensitivity and nurturing
- Using diplomacy and tact
- Being naturally cooperative and supportive

- Showing protective instincts and loyalty
- Having natural charisma and magnetism

Leadership & Professional Abilities:

- Having strong teaching and speaking skills
- Being naturally articulate and authoritative
- Excellence at delegating and networking
- Making decisions with purpose
- Working efficiently and quickly
- Being dependable and responsible
- Maintaining natural professionalism

Transformative & Spiritual Qualities:

- Natural healing and counselling abilities
- Having a catalytic presence that sparks change
- Showing deep emotional intelligence
- Expressing spiritual awareness
- Ability to bring people together
- Being naturally appreciative and discerning
- Creating peace and harmony

Creative & Dynamic Traits:

- Being innovative and pioneering
- Thinking visionary and expansively
- Showing natural adventure and dynamism
- Expressing energy and enthusiasm
- Being creative and resourceful
- Showing versatility and uniqueness
- Being naturally demonstrative and expressive

Adaptability & Wisdom:

- Being flexible and adaptable
- Showing patience and calmness
- Maintaining open-mindedness and astuteness
- Thinking practically and objectively
- Having clear and rational thought
- Possessing deep knowledge and expertise
- Being consistent and reliable

As you heal your emotional baggage, you will discover that many of the strengths you have used for protection are actually your true gifts in disguise. The difference is that instead of using them reactively from a place of fear, you will begin expressing them freely from a place of choice and authenticity. Your protection system has been preserving these gifts all along, waiting for the moment when you feel safe enough to share them with the world in their purest form.

Your Struggles & Life Lessons

We each come into this life with certain themes that we are meant to encounter, understand, and overcome. Life has a way of presenting us with the same challenges over and over - not to make things harder, but to show us what we need to heal. These recurring patterns are not punishments. Instead, they are signposts pointing to the emotional baggage we are carrying and the areas where we have an opportunity to grow. Perhaps you continue to face situations that test your trust, or maybe you repeatedly encounter opportunities to find your voice.

Consider these struggles as life lessons. When you look closely, you will often notice:

- certain themes that keep appearing in your relationships
- challenges that seem to follow you from situation to situation
- areas where you are continually pushed to grow
- patterns that repeat until you learn what they are teaching
- wisdom you are gaining through these experiences

Each challenge brings an opportunity to develop a deeper understanding and self-awareness. These lessons are not random difficulties - they are carefully designed pathways to becoming more fully yourself. The wisdom you gain through facing these challenges becomes part of your unique contribution to the world.

What is important to understand is that when you truly learn the lesson behind your struggles, the pattern will stop repeating itself. The head-to-heart healing process we explored in the chapter on emotional baggage is one powerful way to achieve this transformation. When you genuinely take on board the wisdom of your struggles, you will notice that those particular challenges will no longer keep reappearing in your life. Instead of facing the same lesson in different forms, you will be free to move forward. This is how you know you have truly healed and learned what that particular struggle was meant to teach you.

Your Purpose & Path

Your purpose is not just about what you do - it is about the unique way you are meant to contribute to the world. It is where your essence, gifts, and life lessons come together to create something meaningful. It is your soul's way of making its mark on the world.

Your purpose might show up as:

- a consistent theme in how you naturally help others
- a particular type of change you create in situations
- a special way you impact relationships
- a unique perspective you bring to challenges
- a specific problem you feel deeply called to solve
- a form of contribution that energises rather than drains you

Think of your purpose as the intersection of your authentic gifts and the world's needs. It is not necessarily about your job or career (though it can express itself through your work). It is about the particular way you are designed to make a difference. When you are living your purpose, you will often find that:

- your natural gifts flow easily into service
- your life lessons provide wisdom that helps others
- your essence shines through in everything you do
- your contribution feels both meaningful and natural

Remember, your purpose is not something you need to figure out intellectually - you uncover by paying attention to what naturally calls to you, what problems you feel drawn to solve, and what kind of difference you want to make in the world. It is about aligning your outer actions with your inner truth and allowing your unique contribution to emerge naturally.

The Symphony of Your Soul Signature

This is about recognising the unique combination of qualities that make you distinctly you. These elements are not separate pieces - they are intertwined aspects of your Soul Signature that work together to create the remarkable individual you are.

Your essence naturally influences how you express your gifts. Perhaps your nurturing nature shapes how you lead, or your analytical mind influences how you create. The challenges you have faced are not just obstacles to get past - they are experiences that have given you unique wisdom. When you heal from these struggles, you gain insights that can help others going through similar situations. By combining your natural talents with the wisdom you have gained from your life experiences, you discover your own special way of making a difference in the world.

Like a symphony, your essence is the underlying melody; your gifts are the individual instruments. Your life lessons provide the depth and complexity, and your purpose is the complete musical piece that emerges when everything is in harmony. When these elements align, you experience a sense of flow and rightness that tells you that you are on your personal path.

Notice how these different elements already show up in your life. Pay attention to the moments when you feel most naturally yourself, the challenges that keep appearing for your growth, and the ways you are drawn to contribute. Because understanding your Soul Signature is not about becoming someone new - it is about embracing and expressing more fully the person you already are.

Living as the Real You

Throughout history, wisdom traditions have recognised a profound truth: living authentically is not just about feeling happy - it is about flourishing by being true to your deepest nature. The ancient Greeks called this way of being 'eudaimonia' (pronounced 'you-die-moh-nee-uh'), and their understanding of it offers valuable insights for our own journey of becoming more fully ourselves.

Think of eudaimonia as what happens when you align your outer life with your Soul Signature. It is not about chasing temporary pleasures or achieving specific goals. Instead, it is about creating a life that expresses who you truly are. When you live this way, you don't just feel good occasionally - you experience a deeper sense of rightness and purpose in everything you do.

This way of living touches every part of your life. It shows in how you make choices, build relationships, and contribute to the world. Rather than just going through the motions or following others' expectations, you actively engage with life from your authentic centre. You develop your natural gifts, learn from your challenges, and express your unique purpose.

Living this way means honouring all aspects of who you are. You are not just your job, your roles, or your achievements - you are a whole person with physical, emotional, intellectual, and spiritual dimensions. True flourishing comes from nurturing all these parts of yourself and allowing them to work together in harmony.

Most importantly, this journey is not about reaching some final destination where everything is perfect. It is an ongoing process of discovery and growth. Each challenge presents an opportunity to gain a deeper understanding of yourself. Each setback presents an opportunity to align more closely with your authentic nature.

When you embrace this path, something remarkable happens. Instead of exhausting yourself trying to be who others want you to be, you find deep satisfaction in expressing your true self. Your relationships become more genuine, your work more meaningful, and your contribution to the world more natural and impactful. This is what it means to truly flourish - not by becoming someone else, but by being more fully who you already are.

The Real You Versus the Conditioned You

Let us explore the differences between living authentically as yourself and operating from our conditioned patterns. Understanding these contrasts can help you recognise when you are aligned with your true self versus when you are caught in old patterns.

- *Being vs Doing*: At your core, authentic living flows from simply being who you are. When caught in the false self, you become trapped in a constant state of doing, trying to earn your place in the world.
- *Soul Signature vs Persona*: Living authentically means expressing your natural way of being. When you live from the false self, you maintain a persona—a mask designed to win approval or avoid rejection.
- *Truth vs Image*: When you live authentically, you stay true to yourself and create genuine connections with others. Living from the false self means maintaining an image, which only leads to surface-level relationships.
- *Inward vs Outward Focus*: When you are living as your real self, your attention naturally turns inward, guided by your inner wisdom and truth. The false self keeps looking outward, constantly seeking validation and direction from others.
- *Integration vs Fragmentation*: Your real self moves toward wholeness, bringing together all aspects of who you are.

The false self stays fragmented, hiding away parts that do not fit its ideal image.

- *Wholeness vs Division*: Living authentically means embracing your complete self, including your imperfections. When you live from the false self, you create internal division by rejecting parts of yourself that do not match your imagined standards.
- *Depth vs Shallow*: Your real self naturally moves toward depth in relationships and experiences. The false self keeps you in shallow waters, avoiding real vulnerability.
- *Connection vs Isolation*: When you live authentically, you create genuine connections through honest expression. Living from the false self often leaves you feeling isolated, even in relationships, because others never see the real you.
- *Flow vs Force*: Your real self moves with life's natural flow, even through difficult times. The false self tries to force outcomes, constantly struggling against what is.
- *Alignment vs Adaptation*: Living authentically means staying aligned with your truth. You constantly adapt to meet others' expectations when you are in your false self.
- *Gifts vs Competencies*: Your real self naturally expresses your innate gifts - those unique qualities that flow effortlessly from who you are. The false self relies heavily on learned competencies and skills you have developed, mainly to prove your worth or gain acceptance.
- *Inspiration vs Motivation*: Your real self moves from inspiration - that deep inner knowing that energises and guides you naturally. The false self depends on motivation, pushing yourself to meet external expectations through willpower and force.
- *Purpose vs Achievement*: When living authentically, you follow a more profound sense of purpose that brings meaning to everything you do. The false self chases after achievements and recognition, seeking worth through external accomplishments.
- *Aspirations vs Goals*: Your authentic aspirations come from your soul's natural yearning for expression and growth. Goals often come from the false self's need to prove its worth or to meet others' expectations.
- *Presence vs Appearance*: Your real self naturally radiates presence - the quality of being fully here, in this moment. The false self remains focused on appearances, constantly concerned about how things appear to others.
- *Thrive vs Survive*: Your real self naturally moves toward

what helps you thrive and grow. When you are in your false self, you operate from survival mode, doing whatever it takes to stay safe or fit in.
- *Fulfilment vs Success*: Living authentically brings deep fulfilment from being true to yourself. When you chase external success from your false self, you will find it never quite satisfies.

Remember, we all move between these different ways of being - it is part of the human experience. The goal is not perfection but awareness. Each time you notice yourself operating from the false self, you can choose again - to take a breath, reconnect with your truth, and let more of your authentic self guide the way.

Your journey is not about eliminating the false self; it is about gradually letting more of your true self lead your life. As you practice this awareness, you will naturally move toward more authentic ways of being, one choice at a time.

Tune into how these different ways of being feel in your body and life. Notice which choices bring you more energy and which leave you drained. Let this awareness guide you toward living more fully as your authentic self.

Aligning Your Desires and Actions with Your Soul

When you connect deeply with your authentic self, a profound shift occurs in how you relate to your desires and dreams. Instead of wanting things to prove your worth or meet others' expectations, your aspirations naturally align with who you truly are.

Think about something you have been dreaming of - perhaps a new home or career move. As the real you, notice how your relationship with these desires transforms. That home you envision becomes less about status and more about creating a space for being yourself and meaningful connections. Your career aspirations shift from climbing the corporate ladder to finding ways to share your unique gifts.

Holding Dreams Lightly

Think about holding a beautiful butterfly. If you grasp it too tightly, you will crush it. If you do not create space for it to land, you will never experience its beauty. This is precisely how to hold your dreams and aspirations.

This approach is called non-attachment. It does not mean not caring or not having desires. Instead, it is about:

- holding your dreams with open hands rather than closed fists
- staying flexible about how your aspirations might show themselves
- finding contentment in the journey rather than fixating on the destination
- focusing on the essence of what you want rather than its exact form

For example, instead of saying, 'I must have this specific job,' hold the intention, 'I want to use my gifts to make a meaningful difference.' This flexibility allows life to surprise you with possibilities even better than you imagined.

Understanding Inspired Action

There is a profound difference between taking action because you think you should and moving forward because you are genuinely inspired. When you act from inspiration:

- you move from inner guidance rather than external pressure
- you feel energised even when working hard
- you experience more flow and synchronicity
- you find joy in the process itself

You will know you are taking inspired action by paying attention to how it feels in your body and spirit. When you are aligned with inspiration, you will feel a natural inner pull toward something, accompanied by genuine enthusiasm and energy. Even without knowing all the steps ahead, you will experience a sense of clarity about the direction you are moving in. Perhaps most tellingly, you will feel a deep sense of rightness about your actions, even when challenges arise.

To cultivate more of this inspired action in your life, start by paying close attention to your energy. Notice what naturally draws you and gives you energy, versus what drains you. Trust your inner sense of timing rather than forcing things to happen on a set schedule. Begin with small steps, knowing you don't need to see the whole path ahead to start moving forward. Stay flexible and open to unexpected opportunities that may arise along the way. And during quieter periods when inspiration isn't immediately apparent, focus on simply being, rather than pushing yourself to do. These moments of stillness often create space for fresh inspiration to emerge.

Remember, inspiration is not about waiting for perfect conditions. It is about tuning into your authentic self and moving forward in alignment with your true nature. Even when work is challenging, there is an underlying sense of rightness when acting from inspiration.

Trust that the right paths will continue to open before you as you stay aligned with your authentic self. Your job is not to force or control this unfolding - it is to stay true to who you are and take inspired action when it feels right. Sometimes, the most minor authentic choice leads to the most profound transformation.

THE JOURNEY OF REBECOMING

'The privilege of a lifetime is to become who you truly are.' - Carl Jung

Think of your life as a single day—with a morning, high noon, an afternoon, and an evening. This journey of rebecoming is not about starting over, but rather about moving naturally from one phase to the next, each with its own purpose and gifts. In this final chapter, we will revisit everything you have learned throughout this book, using this metaphor of life's daily cycle to illuminate how the challenges of your morning, the awakening of high noon, and the wisdom of afternoon all work together in your journey back to your authentic self.

The Morning of Your Life is When You build your Place in the World

The morning of your life is about establishing yourself in the world. During this time, you build your identity through achievements, roles, and meeting expectations. You develop your career, form relationships, and create a place for yourself in society. This is necessary and important work.

In these morning hours, you learn the rules of the game. You figure out how to succeed according to society's definitions. You collect credentials, build a career, perhaps start a family, and buy a home. You chase promotions, recognition, or status symbols that show you're 'making it.'

This morning phase serves an essential purpose—it helps you develop skills, discipline, and the capacity to function in the world. The ego you build during this time is not your enemy; it is a necessary structure that allows you to navigate life's complexities.

The Morning's Challenges

But as we explored in Part 1 of this book, the morning phase often brings challenges that can hold you back from your authentic self:

- You have not yet discovered the true cost of avoiding responsibility. Blaming others, making excuses, and seeing yourself as a victim keeps you powerless. Until you own your choices and responses, you remain stuck in patterns that do not serve you.

- Past wounds, traumas, and unprocessed emotions weigh you down like invisible luggage. Your protection system—the Wolf, Bear, and other defensive parts—works overtime to keep you safe from pain, but in doing so, limits your growth and authentic expression.
- Society, media, family expectations, and cultural programming shape your thoughts and behaviours without your conscious awareness. You live according to others' scripts rather than your own truth, not yet recognising how deeply conditioning controls your choices.
- Morning's version of love is conditional, fear-based, and transactional. You confuse attachment with love, need with desire, and approval with acceptance. True heart-based, unconditional love remains foreign to you.
- You pour yourself out for others while running on empty. Self-care feels selfish or indulgent rather than essential. You have not learned that caring for yourself is the foundation for genuinely caring for others.
- Your relationship with money is fraught with fear, scarcity thinking, and inherited beliefs. Money becomes either an obsession or something you avoid, but never a neutral tool for creating value and supporting your authentic path.
- Without energetic boundaries or clearing practices, you absorb others' emotions and the collective stress around you. This accumulated negativity depletes your vitality and clouds your natural joy.
- These complementary masculine and feminine energies within you are at war. You overidentify with one while suppressing the other, creating an internal imbalance that manifests as burnout, disconnection, or unfulfillment.
- Despite checking all the boxes society says should make you happy, a void persists within. This emptiness—actually your soul calling you home—drives you to seek more external achievements that never satisfy.

These morning challenges are not failures—they are natural parts of establishing yourself in the world. But as the sun rises higher in the sky, something begins to shift.

High Noon is the Pivotal Turning Point

High noon is that crucial moment when you realise the morning's approach is no longer working. It is when you ask yourself: 'Is this all there is?' Even with all your achievements, something feels off.

This moment of reckoning can come as a midlife crisis, a health scare, a relationship breakdown, or simply as a growing sense of emptiness that cannot be filled by more of what worked in the morning. For some, it arrives as a sudden awakening. For others, it is a gradual awareness that stretches over months or years.

If you are reading this book, you have likely heard the call of high noon. And we want to acknowledge the courage that it takes. Many people sense this turning point but choose to ignore it. They double down on morning strategies, seeking more achievements, more recognition, more external validation—hoping that just a little more will finally fill that emptiness.

But you have chosen a different path. You have chosen to heed the call, even though it might mean questioning everything you have built so far. That takes real bravery.

As Carl Jung wisely noted, 'We cannot live the afternoon of life according to the programme of life's morning, for what was great in the morning will be little at evening and what in the morning was true, at evening will have become a lie.'

The Afternoon of Your Life is When You Begin to Live as the Real You

As the sun begins its afternoon journey, you are called to turn inward. Through the transformative work of Part 3, you have begun shifting from morning's external focus to afternoon's inner wisdom:

- You have practised taking full responsibility for your life through the exercises. No longer playing the victim, you now understand that while you cannot control what happens to you, you always have the power to control your response. This ownership has become your source of authentic power.
- You have recognised the conditioning that shaped your morning and practised standing in your own truth. The validation you once sought externally now comes from within. Others' opinions no longer dictate your choices—you have reclaimed your authentic voice.
- Through the Head-to-Heart Healing practices, you have identified and begun releasing the wounds your protection system guarded. Your Wolf's hypervigilance relaxes, your Bear's reactive rescuing eases, as you have

healed what they were protecting. The exercises helped you move from intellectual understanding to genuine emotional release.

- Your daily practice of self-love has transformed how you relate to yourself and others. You now embody the difference between conditional, mind-based love and unconditional, heart-based love. Choosing love over fear has become natural for you. You have discovered what dogs always knew—presence without conditions.
- Self-care is no longer an afterthought but your foundation. Through consistent practice, you have learned to replenish before you are depleted. Your inner dialogue has shifted from criticism to compassion. You treat yourself with the kindness you would show a beloved friend.
- Working through your money story exercises has healed old wounds around worth and scarcity. Financial serenity practices have replaced money anxiety. You now experience money as a tool for creating value, not a measure of your worth. The middle way with money feels natural.
- Using energy practices, you have learned to clear what drains you and cultivate what energises you. Morning rituals, energetic boundaries, and clearing techniques have restored your natural vitality. You now recognise and protect yourself from energy vampires.
- Through integration exercises, you have begun healing the inner divide. The masculine's presence and purpose now dance with the feminine's intuition and flow. This inner marriage creates wholeness where division once reigned.
- You've awakened your inner Owl - that wise part of you that sees clearly. Through your Soul Signature work, you've discovered who you truly are at your core, identified your natural gifts that come easily to you, and learned to see the wisdom hidden in your struggles. Your unique purpose has emerged naturally from all of this. Now, moment by moment, you can tell the difference between your true self and those old patterns you picked up along the way. You're no longer constantly doing and achieving - you're simply being who you are. Instead of performing for others, you're present and real. Instead of just chasing success, you're finding true fulfilment. From this place, the right actions flow naturally because you're aligned with who you truly are.

Living Your Afternoon Wisdom

As you continue practising what you have learned, these shifts deepen:

- Morning's limited identity dissolves as you embody your expanded self.
- Protective patterns relax as your gentle Deer play freely.
- Your Raven's anxiety transforms into focused creativity.
- Authentic choices become second nature.
- Your presence naturally uplifts others.
- Life flows with less effort, more grace.

Challenges still arise, but you meet them with afternoon wisdom—seeing growth opportunities rather than threats to who you are.

Your Journey Continues

Remember that afternoon does not reject morning—it builds upon it. Everything you learned and created in the morning remains valuable, but now serves a deeper purpose aligned with your authentic self.

The journey from morning to afternoon is not about abandoning achievements but finding their true meaning. It is about integrating all you have learned into a more whole expression of who you are.

You have everything you need within you:

- your unique gifts waiting to be expressed
- wisdom gained from morning's experiences
- your natural way of being in the world
- the courage to follow your authentic path

As you move through the afternoon, let the real you lead the way. Trust that your inner wisdom will guide you toward what is truly best.

The Evening Horizon

As you continue through the afternoon, you may begin to catch a glimpse of the evening to come. This is not an ending but a further deepening—a time when boundaries soften between self and others, between inner and outer worlds.

In evening's light, you participate fully in life while standing on the foundation of afternoon wisdom. The struggles that once consumed your morning hours are seen with completely new eyes. You recognise life's patterns and purpose for what they are, engaging with them lightly, with joy rather than attachment.

Evening brings a profound integration where:

- your individual journey merges with the collective whole
- personal wisdom becomes universal understanding
- the need to strive dissolves into simple being
- love expands beyond personal to encompass all

You will know evening approaches when meaningful peace and contentment become your natural state. Difficulties do not vanish, but you move through them guided by wisdom so deep it feels like grace rather than effort.

The Path Ahead

We are all on this path together, moving through our own days at our own pace. Some are navigating the morning's challenges, others are hearing the call of high noon, many are embracing the afternoon's transformation, and some are glimpsing the evening's transcendent wisdom.

By embracing each phase—morning's necessary building, afternoon's authentic becoming, and evening's ultimate integration—you honour the fullness of human experience. You are not just changing; you are participating in the eternal rhythm of growth and return.

This journey continues to unfold, revealing new depths of who you truly are with each passing hour. The privilege of a lifetime awaits—to rebecome who you truly are.

APPENDIX: THE SCIENCE BEHIND THE HEAD-TO-HEART HEALING METHODS & PRACTICES

The Head-to-Heart Healing approach presented in this book is grounded in decades of scientific research from psychology, neuroscience, and clinical studies. While these practices have ancient roots in wisdom, modern science has begun to validate many of their mechanisms and effectiveness. This appendix provides an overview of the research supporting each method, helping you understand why these approaches work and giving you confidence in their application.

Understanding The Research Landscape

Before diving into specific methods, it is important to understand that research in emotional healing exists on a spectrum. Some approaches have extensive empirical support with multiple randomised controlled trials, while others are based on established psychological principles but need more specific research. We have organised the methods according to their current level of scientific validation.

Extensively Research-Supported Methods

Discovery Writing Method

Research Foundation: Dr James Pennebaker's groundbreaking research programme, beginning in 1986, represents one of the most robust bodies of evidence in the field of emotional healing research.

Key Findings:

- Over 20 studies demonstrate significant physical and psychological health benefits
- Participants show reduced doctor visits, improved immune function, and better psychological well-being
- Effect sizes are comparable to those found in major medical advances
- Benefits include reduced symptoms of anxiety, depression, and PTSD
- Physical improvements include better sleep, lower blood pressure, and enhanced immune response

How It Works: Research suggests that translating emotional

experiences into words changes how memories are organised in the brain. Neuroimaging studies show that this method of writing activates areas associated with emotional processing while reducing activation in stress-response regions. The act of writing appears to help integrate traumatic memories, thereby reducing their emotional charge.

Clinical Applications: Expressive writing has been successfully used with diverse populations, including college students, trauma survivors, patients with chronic pain, and healthcare workers. Studies consistently show that 15-20 minutes of writing for 3-4 consecutive days can produce lasting benefits.

Mindfulness-Based Approaches

Research Foundation: Thousands of studies have examined mindfulness and its applications in emotional regulation, with particularly strong evidence for its role in trauma recovery and emotional healing.

Key Findings:

- Neuroimaging studies show mindfulness increases activity in prefrontal cortex regions responsible for emotional regulation
- Reduces amygdala reactivity (the brain's alarm system) during emotional challenges
- Improves emotional recovery time and reduces emotional intensity
- Enhances present-moment awareness and reduces rumination
- Shows significant benefits for anxiety, depression, and PTSD symptoms

How It Works: Mindfulness appears to work through multiple mechanisms. It strengthens top-down emotional regulation by enhancing prefrontal cortex function while simultaneously reducing bottom-up emotional reactivity. Regular practice literally changes brain structure, increasing grey matter in areas associated with emotional regulation and decreasing it in stress-response regions.

Clinical Evidence: Mindfulness-Based Stress Reduction (MBSR) and Mindfulness-Based Cognitive Therapy (MBCT) have been extensively validated in clinical settings. Research shows these approaches are as effective as traditional therapies for many conditions, with the added benefit of teaching skills for ongoing self-regulation.

Body Awareness and Somatic Approaches (Feeling What You've Been Avoiding)

Research Foundation: The field of somatic therapy, particularly Somatic Experiencing, has begun to build a solid research base, with the first randomised controlled trial published in 2017.

Key Findings:

- Somatic Experiencing shows statistically significant reductions in PTSD symptoms
- Body-based approaches are effective for both traumatised and non-traumatised populations
- Improvements include reduced anxiety, depression, and somatic symptoms
- Benefits extend to overall life quality and emotional regulation
- Particularly effective for trauma that traditional talk therapies struggle to address

How It Works: Trauma research shows that traumatic experiences are stored not just in memory but in the body's nervous system. Somatic approaches work by helping individuals develop awareness of internal sensations (interoception) and using this awareness to complete interrupted defensive responses. This bottom-up processing complements traditional top-down cognitive approaches.

Neuroscience Support: Brain imaging studies indicate that body-focused interventions activate distinct neural pathways compared to purely cognitive approaches, engaging areas associated with embodied awareness and emotional processing. This may explain why some individuals benefit more from somatic approaches than traditional talk therapy.

Forgiveness-Based Interventions

Research Foundation: Forgiveness research has grown exponentially over the past three decades, with multiple systematic reviews and meta-analyses confirming its therapeutic value.

Key Findings:

- Forgiveness therapy significantly reduces anger, anxiety, and depression
- Increases hope, self-esteem, and overall psychological

well-being

- Physical health benefits include reduced heart attack risk, improved cholesterol levels, better sleep, and lower blood pressure
- Effects are maintained over time and appear to strengthen with practice
- Benefits occur regardless of whether reconciliation with the offender takes place

How It Works: Neuroimaging studies show that forgiveness activates brain networks associated with empathy, perspective-taking, and emotional regulation. The process appears to help individuals reframe or reevaluate harmful events in ways that reduce their emotional impact. Forgiveness does not require forgetting or condoning harmful behaviour—rather, it involves releasing the emotional charge associated with past hurts.

Clinical Applications: Process-based forgiveness interventions (like the approaches described in this book) have been successfully used with diverse populations, including abuse survivors, ex-service personnel, and individuals dealing with relationship conflicts. The structured nature of these interventions makes them particularly effective.

Self-Reflection and Self-Inquiry Methods

Research Foundation: Self-reflection has been extensively studied in therapeutic, educational, and professional development contexts, with robust evidence for its benefits.

Key Findings:

- Self-reflection improves empathy, emotional regulation, and interpersonal skills
- Enhances problem-solving abilities and learning from experience
- Increases self-awareness and emotional intelligence
- Improves therapeutic outcomes when used by healthcare providers
- Associated with better workplace performance and job satisfaction

How It Works: Self-reflection engages metacognitive processes—thinking about thinking—which enables individuals to step back from immediate emotional reactions and gain a more objective perspective. Brain imaging shows that reflective processes activate prefrontal regions associated with executive function and emotional regulation.

Professional Applications: Research in healthcare and therapy training shows that professionals who engage in regular self-reflection show improved empathy, reduced burnout, and better client outcomes. This suggests that self-reflection skills benefit both the practitioner and those they serve.

Moderately Research-Supported Methods

Ho'oponopono (Hawaiian Forgiveness Practice)

Research Foundation: Although Ho'oponopono has limited empirical research, the available studies are promising and align with broader research on forgiveness.

Key Findings:

- One controlled study showed statistically significant reductions in unforgiveness compared to a control group
- Participants reported improved emotional states and a greater sense of peace
- The practice appears to work through similar mechanisms as other forgiveness interventions
- Case reports document improvements in anxiety, depression, and relationship conflicts

Cultural and Clinical Context: Ho'oponopono represents a culturally specific approach to forgiveness that incorporates elements found in evidence-based practices, including acknowledgement of responsibility, expression of remorse, gratitude, and love. While more research is needed, the practice aligns with established principles of emotional healing.

Emerging Approaches Receiving Further Research

Several methods presented in this book, while based on established psychological principles, will be the subject of more specific research:

Mirror Method (Relationship Reflection)

Principle Base: Grounded in attachment theory and the therapeutic concept of projection, where we see aspects of ourselves reflected in our relationships.

Related Research: Studies on couples therapy have shown that self-reflection exercises can increase relationship satisfaction by 80%. Therapeutic mirroring research demonstrates its value in clinical settings.

Heyoka Method (Sacred Mirror Feedback)

Principle Base: Based on Native American wisdom traditions and modern feedback research.

Related Research: Group therapy and feedback interventions have been demonstrated to enhance self-awareness and promote personal growth.

Speak Freely Method (Deep Listening Practice)

Principle Base: Rooted in person-centred therapy principles and listening research.

Related Research: Studies have shown that feeling heard and understood have therapeutic benefits.

Trigger Tracking Method

Principle Base: Based on cognitive-behavioural monitoring techniques and mindfulness principles.

Related Research: CBT monitoring and mindfulness-based approaches have been shown to have documented benefits.

Discovery Drawing Method

Principle Base: Grounded in art therapy research, expressive arts therapy principles, and neurobiological understanding of visual processing and emotional expression.

Related Research: While discovery drawing as a specific structured method requires more direct research, it draws from several well-established research areas:

- Art Therapy Research: Meta-analyses of art therapy interventions show significant benefits for trauma processing, with effect sizes comparable to traditional talk therapies. Studies demonstrate that art-making activates neural pathways distinct from those involved in verbal processing, potentially accessing traumatic memories stored in non-verbal brain regions.
- Visual Expression and Trauma: Neuroimaging research shows that traumatic memories are often stored as sensory fragments rather than coherent narratives. Visual expression can access these fragmented

memories more directly than verbal approaches, particularly for pre-verbal trauma or experiences that overwhelm language capacity.
- Colour Psychology and Emotion: Research demonstrates consistent cross-cultural associations between colours and emotions (red with anger/energy, blue with sadness/calm), suggesting that colour choice in drawing can provide valid emotional information. Studies show that individuals unconsciously select colours that reflect their emotional states.
- Bilateral Brain Engagement: The physical act of drawing engages both hemispheres of the brain simultaneously, similar to bilateral stimulation techniques used in EMDR. Research suggests this bilateral activation may facilitate trauma processing and emotional integration.
- Non-Verbal Processing Benefits: Studies with individuals who have alexithymia (difficulty identifying and describing emotions) show that visual expression methods can be more effective than verbal approaches. This suggests particular value for those who struggle with expressing emotions in writing or verbally.

Emerging Evidence: Case studies from art therapy journals document the effectiveness of time-limited drawing exercises for emotional processing. The 20-minute structure aligns with research on the optimal duration for emotional processing tasks, striking a balance between sufficient engagement and avoiding overwhelm.

Clinical Context: The method's emphasis on continuous movement and non-judgmental expression aligns with established principles of expressive therapy. The structured time frame and focus on process over product mirror evidence-based approaches in art therapy, which emphasise the healing value of the creative process itself rather than the artistic outcome.

Love Letter Method (Self-Compassion Writing)

Principle Base: Grounded in self-compassion research and therapeutic letter-writing techniques.

Related Research: Self-compassion interventions show significant benefits for mental health and emotional regulation.

Raven Method (Evidence Gathering for New Beliefs)

Principle Base: Based on cognitive restructuring principles from

CBT.

Related Research: Cognitive restructuring techniques have extensive research support.

--

IMPORTANT CONSIDERATIONS

Individual Differences

Studies consistently show that different approaches are more effective for different individuals. Factors that may influence effectiveness include:

- Personality traits (particularly openness to experience and emotional expressiveness)
- Cultural background and spiritual beliefs
- Type and timing of traumatic experiences
- Current life circumstances and support systems
- Previous therapy experience

Integration with Professional Care

While these methods can be powerful tools for healing, you should seek professional mental health care when needed. Research shows that self-help approaches work best when:

- Used as part of a comprehensive approach to healing
- Combined with appropriate professional support for complex trauma
- Practised consistently over time rather than as one-time interventions
- Adapted to individual needs and circumstances

The Importance of Safety

All trauma-informed approaches emphasise the importance of emotional safety. If any method feels overwhelming or activates intense reactions, it is important to:

- Slow down or pause the process
- Seek professional support
- Remember that healing is not linear
- Practice self-compassion throughout the journey

FUTURE DIRECTIONS

The field of trauma and emotional healing continues to evolve rapidly. Emerging areas of research include:

- Epigenetics and how healing practices may influence gene expression
- The role of the nervous system in trauma storage and release
- Integration of ancient wisdom practices with modern neuroscience
- Personalised approaches based on individual trauma histories and neural patterns
- Technology-assisted interventions and their effectiveness

Conclusion

The Head-to-Heart Healing approach represents a bridge between ancient wisdom and modern science. While some methods have extensive research validation, others are based on well-established principles that show promise for future validation. The integration of multiple approaches—addressing cognitive, emotional, somatic, and spiritual dimensions of healing—aligns with the current understanding of trauma as a whole-person experience that requires whole-person healing.

As you work with these methods, remember that you are participating in an ongoing dialogue between traditional healing wisdom and scientific understanding. Trust your experience while remaining open to professional support when needed. The goal is not perfect implementation but rather finding the approaches that resonate with your unique healing journey.

Most importantly, remember that seeking healing takes courage. Whether a method has decades of research behind it or represents an emerging approach, your willingness to engage in this work is itself a significant step toward emotional freedom and authentic living.

For readers interested in exploring the research in greater detail, we recommend consulting the original studies and systematic reviews. Many are available through academic databases, and some authors maintain websites with accessible summaries of their work.

ABOUT THE AUTHORS

Cilla Hall

Cilla's career spans property management, recruitment, HR, administration, and interior design. As a qualified life coach, she combines business skills with a deep understanding of human potential. Her creative talents led her to run a successful personalised gifts and greetings cards business.

In 2013, Cilla co-founded Wellspring Academy, an innovative school programme giving struggling students a fresh start. She is the author of the *Little Book of Choices.*

Steve Roche

Steve's first entry into the field of emotional well-being was as one of the original directors of Kooth, the UK's leading digital mental health services provider. The multiple-award company pioneered online counselling back in 2004 and listed on the London Stock Exchange in 2020. Steve is also one of the country's most experienced business plan writers and startup consultants.

Beyond his business endeavours, he co-founded a pioneering school-within-a-school in 2013. As a volunteer, Steve led one of the UK's largest grassroots football clubs, is a two-time President of West London Speakers and is a former Area Director of Toastmasters International. He has written several books, including The MultipleMind Method and The Power of Masterminding.

ABOUT HEAD, HEART & SOUL

Head, Heart & Soul (www.headheartandsoul.co.uk) is a transformational personal development company founded by Steve Roche and Cilla Hall, co-authors of this book. The company emerged from their own journey of inner work and healing, which began over a decade ago, officially launching only after its founders had personally walked the path they now guide others through.

Their core philosophy centres on the belief that most people have lost touch with their authentic selves through life's accumulated hurts, conditioning, and protective mechanisms, and that true transformation comes from systematically working through nine key life dimensions: taking responsibility, healing emotional baggage, understanding love, self-care, breaking conditioning, financial well-being, energy management, inner balance, and discovering one's soul purpose.

The company offers a comprehensive range of transformation tools, including workshops, retreats, one-on-one guidance sessions, and online resources. Their signature offerings include the 'Breaking Free' emotional healing workshop, 'The Truth About Love' workshop, and 'The Real You' purpose discovery retreat. What sets Head, Heart & Soul apart is its integration of ancient wisdom practices with practical, modern applications, delivered by founders who openly share their own struggles and breakthroughs rather than positioning themselves as gurus.

Operating primarily from London with retreats in the UK countryside and Europe, Head, Heart & Soul has built a community of members actively engaged in the 'Rebecoming' journey. Their approach emphasises that transformation is not about fixing what is broken but about removing the layers that obscure one's true nature. With their combination of group workshops, personal support, and comprehensive resources, they have created a bridge between the life people think they have to live and the authentic life they can actually claim.

www.ingramcontent.com/pod-product-compliance
Lightning Source LLC
LaVergne TN
LVHW051624080426
835511LV00016B/2163

* 9 7 8 1 9 1 6 2 4 9 3 8 7 *